A PHILOSOPHER REFLECTS
ON THE ROSARY

by

RAYMOND DENNEHY

En Route Books and Media, LLC
St. Louis, MO

Make the time

En Route Books and Media, LLC
5705 Rhodes Avenue
St. Louis, MO 63109

Cover credit: Dr. Sebastian Mahfood, OP

Contact us at contactus@enroutebooksandmedia.com

Library of Congress Control Number: 2021933886
ISBN-13: 978-1-952464-64-5

ACKNOWLEDGMENTS

I am indebted to my friend and colleague, John Galten, for urging me to continue to write this book about the Rosary. Absent his urging, there may well not have been any book by me about Mary and the Rosary, even though, while a graduate student, I'd promised our Blessed Mother that I'd write a book on her if I got my Ph.D. in philosophy. I did that, so why my intellectual and volitional paralysis? The possibility that there would be no book, confronted me as I, neither a theologian nor a Mariologist, gasped at the vast inventory of books on Mary and her Rosary. But when Galten told me he thought a philosopher could write on its Mysteries, I suddenly thought, "Bingo!"

I am also indebted to the following people:

The Reverend David Meconi, S.J., Editor of the *Homiletic and Pastoral Review,* for permission to reprint the book's Introduction, and my essays on the 1st Joyous and 1st and 2nd Glorious Mysteries that appeared in the journal (May 18, 2018).

Mary Anne Urlakis, Editor of *The Intermountain Catholic,* for permission to reprint my essay, "The Rosary and Human Progress" (May 1, 1981) as the book's *Prologue.*

Sheila St. John, Executive Director of The *California Association of Natural Family Planning,* for permission to reprint a portion of my essay, "Contraception and Homosexuality" (Summer, 2007).

The Rev. Joseph Fessio, S.J., Chief *Honcho* of Ignatius Press, for permission to reprint a portion of my Introduction from the book, *Christian Married Love.*

The Rev. Tom Davis, Executive Director of the Liberty Institute for Faith & Ethics, which owns the St. John Paul II Lecture Series in Bioethics, for permission to reprint my essay, "The Biological Revolution and the Myth of Prometheus" that appeared in Volume II, Bioethical Issues.

For my wife, Maryann, my best friend in the whole world

ABOUT THE BOOK COVER

It's a picture of me in "Boot Camp" at the United States Navy Training Center in San Diego, Ca., August, 1954. What's it doing on the cover of a book about the Rosary? Enlisting in the Navy changed my life for the better. One of the changes was my commitment, during my last year aboard ship, to pray the Rosary every day, usually at night in by bunk.

CONTENTS

Contents

PROLOGUE

The Rosary and Human Progress

The title of this Prologue will probably raise your eyebrows, especially if you think that the Rosary is a remnant of pre-Vatican II superstition, fit nowadays only for old ladies to while away their hours in the back pews of churches. But if you understand this form of prayer, it will not take you long to see that the title makes a great deal of sense. For if anything characterizes the Rosary, it is the Incarnation: the birth and early life of Christ with Mary and Joseph, his suffering and death, and finally, resurrection and triumph over sin. This Incarnational focus is what ties the Rosary to human progress. It is, perhaps, more than coincidental that Pope St. John Paul II, who did not hesitate to admit that the Rosary was his favorite devotion, wrote his first encyclical, *Redemptor hominis*, dealing with the situation of contemporary man in terms of Christ's Incarnation.

Much of the optimism about progress comes from the mouths of secular humanists, such as Corliss Lamont or B. F. Skinner. Even those who do not accept the humanist philosophy of atheism and materialism, which is to say the vast majority of us, tend to think of human progress in terms of purely material achievements—an increasing Gross National Product, miracle drugs, satellites and spaceships.

Of course, these kinds of things are very important, and you cannot have human progress without them. But the fact remains that human progress is just that – *human* progress – and that means there is more to life than money, health, and efficient transportation.

Secular humanism is aggressively anti-God and anti-immortality, and it has succeeded in driving a wedge between God and man. If you think about it, you will quickly realize how God and religion are being driven out of our lives. Consider our embarrassment in talking about God and our faith in public or praying before our family meal when we have guests at the table who are non-religious. And we must not ignore the unrelenting efforts of the American Civil Liberties Union to convince the courts to stop prayer in schools and to forbid displays of Nativity scenes by public agencies during Christmastime. And all the while, we are less and less outraged by light treatment, if not outright defenses, of abortion, pre-marital sex, homosexuality, transgenderism, and pornography in the media. To be sure, America is not the only country where secularism has found a home. The European nations that fail to mention God in their constitutions are Norway, Luxembourg, Iceland, Italy, Portugal, and Spain and, to boot, God is also absent from the European Union's Constitution. Think of it: God is the Sovereign of the universe, the author of our very being; yet we find ourselves less and less capable of keeping Him in our lives, let alone acknowledging Him in public. On top of all this, it is probably true that modern man suspects that godlessness goes hand-in-hand with intelligence, e.g., with being a great scientist or with the creativity of an original artist, etc.

All of which can easily create the impression, even in the minds of serious Christians, that you cannot properly serve God unless you turn away from the world and that an enthusiasm for worldly things will seduce you into godlessness. But such an impression is certainly anti-Christian; specifically, it is contrary to the doctrine of Christ's Incarnation. It is, in fact, a modern version of the age-old Gnostic heresy that the material world is the source of chaos and evil.

Discoveries in biology, like the DNA code and its workings, new expressions in painting and music, greater prosperity for mankind, the conquest of space and disease, and the realization of a just world order are the ways in which we accept God's invitation to use our wit and responsibility to perfect His universe. As He tells us in *Genesis,* His creation is good and worthy of our serious attention and love. The trick, however, is to bear in mind that we do all this for God as our path to union with Him and not simply for our own gratification.

Failure to understand this leads to entrapment by secular humanism. And it is a trap because by trying to exclude God from our lives and purposes, the progress we seek is illusory. We are made to live for God who loves us, and we cannot find happiness and fulfillment without Him. Three centuries of growing secularism and its tiresome exuberance for progress and liberation have left us enveloped in moral and intellectual darkness and under constant threat of nuclear extermination. Here is where the Rosary can be very helpful to each of us. Because it is focused on the life of Christ, we cannot pray it properly without living more and more in the world and, at the same time, living more and more with God.

For example, in the Joyful Mysteries, we open ourselves to Christ's Incarnation: God becomes man. There can be no more profound expression of God, the Father's, love for us than to send His only Son to become "like us in all things except sin."

These are the ways, then, in which the Rosary is intimately tied to the whole question of human progress. Besides being a powerful source of God's grace and, as Father Garrigou-Lagrange observed, "a school of contemplation," the Rosary is also a remedy for the errors of secular humanism; it is a prayer that affirms the goodness of the world and worldly progress while at the same time opening our minds and hearts evermore to the truth that the world belongs to God and that progress is *true* progress only when it leads to Him.

INTRODUCTION

"I don't know how you'll help me, but I know you will."

Why would a philosopher go to bat for the Rosary? I'd better 'fess up right off. I've never been able to convince myself that I'm a philosopher, even though I own a Ph.D. in that discipline and have taught the subject for 49 years, not to mention publishing books and articles in philosophy. I even enjoy moments of philosophical reflection; you know, that's when you ask yourself questions like "What's the meaning of life?" or "Why do ATMs at drive-thru banks have instructions written in Braille?" All in all, if I don't pass muster as a philosopher, I believe my credentials show that at least I'm not a *poseur*. How about a *wannabe*? I would hope that I'm a respectable distance north of a *wannabe* and just a tad south of a philosopher. I would hope.

How do I measure up when it comes to writing about prayer, let alone about the Rosary? I'm no theologian and hardly a saint. So, my plan for this introduction is to sketch the role of prayer in my family life and then move on to write commentaries of the Rosary's Mysteries.

****

"I don't know how you'll help me, but I know you will." These words concluded a prayer my mother made to Mary

1

as she stood before the picture of *Our Mother of Perpetual Help* that hung on the wall in my parents' bedroom. My mother had no money to buy groceries, and she was praying to Mary for help.

At the time, I was in the Navy. It may have been on the same day—and maybe at the same time ("maybe," because all this happened sixty years ago)—that she prayed to Mary while I was at Sunday Mass on the naval base in Long Beach, California. And if it wasn't also *Mother's Day,* that day was close by. I remember that during the celebration of the Mass I couldn't stop thinking about what a suitable Mother's Day gift might be. I decided to send her a money order instead of my initial choice of flowers.

I'm not sure, but I like to think that on the same day that I sent the money order for $25.00 to my mother *via* Western Union, its San Francisco office informed her over the phone that a money order for her was waiting there. Although memory fails me here, I'm assuming that a business-like Western Union would have been open on Sundays. At all events, whenever my mother did get the call, she went directly to their office and got the money order. Today, $25.00 isn't much, but back then, in terms of mid-1950s buying power, it was a lot more money than it is today.

Was my mother's prayer to Mary the reason that I sent a money order instead of flowers? Or was it coincidence? I can't say for sure, but I strongly suspect that Mary had answered her prayer.

Introduction

Establishing the efficacy of prayer can be a difficult task. For the atheist and the deist, the question of prayer's efficacy is a "no-brainer": since for the atheist there's no God and for the deist God exists, but His infinite, absolutely perfect being renders any awareness of creaturely existence unworthy of Him, so in either case there's no possibility of any divine response. If a prayer seems to have been followed by the result for which we were praying, that's because our praying created a mindset that produced hormonal forces in our body that overcame our illness or gave us a sharper focus on what had to be accomplished in order to get the job promotion or to persuade a family member to enter a drug rehabilitation program, etc.

One who believed in the Christian God could counter such skeptical explanations with the claim that the "mind-set" that causes those things is only the *proximate* cause and that God is its *ultimate* cause. God prefers to act *through* things and events, not *on* them. Yes, establishing the efficacy of prayer *intellectually* can be difficult, but those who pray daily are convinced of its power. However, the reason for their convictions about prayer belong more under the category of *lived experience* than intellectual argument. In Mother Theresa's words, "You cannot learn this from books, you must experience in your life, that whatever you ask Our

Lady she will do…"[1] To repeat my mother's words, "I don't know how you'll help me, but I know you will."

The genius of the Rosary is that its Mysteries start us praying in concrete situations, some of which are, to be sure, singular and have never happened before they did happen and will not happen again: an angel informs Mary that the Holy Spirit has impregnated her, she and Joseph search for their twelve year old son, Jesus, for three days before finding Him lecturing the elders in the temple, and twenty-one years later He is humiliated by a kangaroo court, scourged, covered with spittle, and executed, all in bloody, painful fashion. And three days after, God, the Father, raises Him from the dead!

Yet, despite the singularity of these events, they remain sufficiently concrete and "everyday" to draw us into their *human* drama: e.g., unexpected or undesired pregnancy, a lost or wayward child, false accusation of criminal behavior, torture and execution, becoming more Christlike in daily life, helping our neighbor in need despite our own problems, and so forth.

---

[1] María Ruiz Scaperlanda, *Day by Day with María.* "Small Mercies Miércoles: I'm grateful for… Our Lady of Confidence" (March 26, 2014). https://daybydaywithmaria.blogspot.com/2014/03/small-mercies-miercoles-im-grateful-for.html

At the same time, such confrontation with concrete, human events can lead us to *transcend* the concrete and "everyday" to a meditation on how the meaning of Christ's birth affirms the dignity of all human life and how our ability to procreate human beings reveals God's desire that we emulate His creative power and share His parental love and care for them. Moreover, praying the Rosary can lead us to an even higher form of prayer, *Contemplation:* simply being with God, with Christ or Mary as one recites the Lord's Prayer, Hail Mary, and Glory be to the Father.

I grew up in a home where prayer—especially the Rosary—was regarded as important. In the evenings, as we sat in our living room watching television, my Father would go into my parents' bedroom, around 8 PM, to pray his Rosary before returning to resume watching television. My Mother would wait and pray her Rosary in bed. I prayed the Rosary sporadically, usually when I wanted some "important" favor. But, in the last of my four years in the Navy, I started praying my Rosary every night. (Hence, the picture of me on the cover of this book: a sailor in the U.S. Navy.) The years have passed since that auspicious beginning and, thanks to the grace of God, I'm still praying it. My wife, Maryann, joins me.

Since the title of this book promises discussion about how a philosopher regards his Rosary, I want to make clear that, given what I say in the above paragraphs, it might be supposed that I'm "going to bat" for that devotion because it sharpens the philosopher's store of philosophical concepts. *That* too, but my primary purpose in going to bat for the Rosary is more fundamental: Prayer is ultimately the desire to be with God. Prayer is also how we ask God to fulfill our needs and desires, as well as to ask forgiveness for our sins. What it comes down to is that prayer is our confession of ultimate *helplessness*. Consider, for example, Lindsay Eastridge's account of Galileo at prayer:

> In 1582, while praying in a chapel, Galileo observed a lamplighter lighting the chandeliers. The lamplighter would pull the lamps nearer him with a rod, and after lighting them, let them swing until they hung in place. Timing the swings against his own heartbeat, Galileo discovered the law of the pendulum. No matter how wide the arc the lamps made, the time it took to complete a cycle, swinging from one side to the other was the same, even as the size of the arc decreased.[2]

The point I wish to make here is that Galileo was *praying* in a sacred place. That he happened also to discover the "law of the pendulum" while praying may or may not have been accidental. Even if he were praying to discover what governs the *to* and *fro* motion of pendulums, his prayer did not differ

---

[2] Lindsay Eastridge, "Galileo Galilei (1564-1642)." https://www.math.wichita.edu/history/men/galileo.html

in form from my Mother's prayer to Mary for grocery money: Each was asking for Divine assistance. Galileo, the scientist, was *praying for God's help!* Under different circumstances, he might have found himself praying to God for grocery money. Scientists need food, too.

The book's *angle*. I use the Rosary's Mysteries to address our day-to-day challenges. Of course, as I already noted, the Mysteries call our attention to events, some of which happened once and will never happen again. But these events speak to us in ways that transcend time and place. To be sure, so do the writings of the ancients, and that's why they are called "classics." After all, we've learned a lot about how to respond to today's challenges from Plato and Aristotle, the Stoics and Cicero, plus a long list of others who wrote in the past. The difference is that the Mysteries explicitly show, in a concrete and human way, the hand of God in our daily lives, not to mention giving us the ultimate word in how to behave.

Then, there's the *Hypostatic Union*. God, the Son, chose to become a human being without any dilution of His Divinity or any dilution of His human nature: two natures, the Divine and the Human, but only one Divine Person. If, on the contrary, the Second Person of the Trinity had multiplied into two persons, then His relation to human nature would have been purely transcendental: His agony in Gethsemane, suffering and crucifixion, would all have been a sham—hardly something in which God would engage. It would be like someone who leaves a dwelling when its lease expires for better accommodations. We can't understand how Christ can be both God and man in only one Divine Person, but its significance for us is magnificent beyond all description. Imagine: God so loves us that He chose to become our fellow human being, our brother. He could have come down from Heaven as an adult human being, suffered and died for us, and then gone back to heaven as quickly as He had arrived. But, no; to repeat what was said above, He chose to take the long, scenic tour from zygote to fetus, to infant, to adolescent and adult. In short, Christ chose to live the full human life; He was "like us in all things except sin."

Perhaps we have become so accustomed to the teaching that God became man that we take the notion of Christ's Incarnation for granted. But when we spend time thinking about what it means, the notion blows the mind! Think of it: Christ as a crying baby, as a child constantly asking his parents, *Why this? Why that?* And as a *teenager!* Think of Christ with His Apostles sitting around a campfire, joking, telling stories, and singing. All this is not only the behavior of a human being, but of God Himself!

JOYFUL MYSTERIES

THE 1ˢᵀ JOYFUL MYSTERY
The Annunciation

My impression is that stories about genies generally have the same theme: the main character finds a bottle, usually buried in the desert sands or hidden in refuse; often, the bottle is not inviting as its smudged with dirt, etc., but its attraction may, for example, be the hope that it contains water that will quench the thirst of the desert wanderer. At all events, when he removes the bottle's lid, a genie pops out who promises to grant his liberator's every wish. How quickly one's life can change for the better! Remarkably, the genie, despite all his miraculous powers, is at the service of whoever happens at the time to possess the bottle.

Our relationship with God is quite different. He is not at our service; we are at His. It's not as if, when finding ourselves in an undesirable situation, we can pull the lid from a bottle and God pops out, ready to make things right. As Jesus tells us, God is our loving Father; being at His service *always* benefits us. But rather than promising to grant our every wish, He often answers our prayers with a big "*No*": Just check out the number of books and articles on the topic, "When God Says No." Christ reminds us that, if we, who are imperfect know how to give good things to our children, how much more does our Father in Heaven know how to give good things to us? God does not cause painful emotional, physical, or financial experiences to enter our lives, but He often *permits* their entry as an opportunity for our spiritual and temporal improvement.

All of which has a direct bearing on Mary's response to God's invitation to her to be the mother of Jesus: Behold the slave girl of the Lord! The abandonment to the Divine Will that she expresses in this response would be lost by interpreting it as an enthusiastic acceptance generated by the prestige of the Divine offer. God created Mary free from Original Sin, so, given the darkening of our understanding and weakening of our will caused by that Sin, is it not plausible to infer that the purity of Mary's desire to serve God and her clarity of intuition of things spiritual, especially of things relating to her mission as the Mother of God (*Theotokos*), surpassed that of all other human beings? Whatever the degree of enthusiasm, her acceptance of God's will sprang from a profound love of, and commitment to, the fulfillment of His will, no matter what He asked of her. Consider what William G. Most writes of Mary's acceptance:

> "'Behold the handmaid of the Lord!' The word *handmaid* is but a poor translation of the original Greek word *doulé*. For to us the word handmaid means merely a hired servant. But *doulé* meant a slave girl. Here is an

obedient humility to balance the proud disobedience of Eve."[3]

Regarding the freedom of Mary's "Yes" to God, St. Luke's passage about the annunciation of the archangel Gabriel to Mary seems to indicate that the Holy Spirit had already impregnated her without her consent. But the Christian tradition gives the passage a different interpretation:

"Many holy fathers (Sts. Jerome, Cyril, Ephrem, Augustine) say that the consent of Mary was essential to the redemption. It was the will of God, St. Thomas says, that the redemption of mankind should depend on the consent of the Virgin Mary. This does not mean that God in His plans was bound by the will of a creature and that man would not have been redeemed if Mary had not consented. It only means that the consent of Mary was foreseen from all eternity and therefore was received as essential in the design of God."[4]

So, when the archangel Gabriel presented Mary with God's invitation to be the mother of Jesus, it was known "from all eternity" that she could have refused; she could

---

[3] William G. Most, *Mary in Our Life.* (Garden City, NY: Image Books, Double Day, 1963), p.31.

[4] New Advent. www.newadvent.org/cathen/01541

have said "No" to God, but she enthusiastically said "Yes": "I am the *slave girl* of the Lord." Looking at the big picture, Christianity is based on personal freedom: God's freedom is absolute, which means that nothing compelled Him to create the universe, let alone the world. As a self-subsisting, absolutely perfect being, He is absolutely self-sufficient and requires nothing other than Himself for his perfect happiness. Because He is absolutely free and self-sufficient, His creation of the world was not inspired by any unfulfilled desire but was instead an act of absolute freedom and perfect love. And because love is the willing of the good of another, it follows that love, absolute and perfect, must be freely given, as well as freely accepted by the beloved: Lucifer could have said "Yes" to God but chose instead to say, "I will not serve." Adam and Eve *de facto* said "No" to God by choosing to eat from the tree of good and evil that He explicitly told them to avoid.

If Mary had not chosen to say "Yes" (*"Behold the Slave Girl of the Lord"*), what would have been the alternatives?

1) God had a "B list" from which He chose another woman who said "Yes"?

2) God repeated his offer to Mary at a later time and she said "Yes"?

3) There would be no Redemption?

14

Fortunately for us, and, as God had seen from eternity, Mary immediately and *freely* accepted the offer to be the mother of Jesus.

The *freedom* of Mary's acceptance deserves a closer look. Like the sea of Homer, *freedom* has many voices. For example, when I was a graduate student and the time had come for me to find a philosophy professor who would direct my doctoral dissertation, I visited the office of the faculty member who taught political philosophy. He asked me on what topic I wished to write my dissertation. "Political Freedom," I replied. His reply to my reply caught me completely off guard: "Mr. Dennehy, the *Syntopicon* of the *Great Books* lists 30 different meanings of 'freedom.' Which meaning did you have in mind?" My reply to his reply? "I'll get back to you on that, Professor."

My review of the various meanings of freedom led me to a renewed appreciation for the classical philosophers' (Socrates, Plato, Aristotle) view that the acquisition of virtue—using free will in accordance with the exigencies of human nature—amplifies one's freedom while the acquisition of vice—using free will in ways that frustrate those exigencies—diminishes it.

For example, in Plato's *Republic,* Socrates claims that doing an injustice harms the one who does the injustice more than the one on whom the injustice is visited. How so? Socrates uses the example of the tyrant who has given in to his base desires—greed, lust, anger, etc.—so often that he no longer has control over them. These vices, moreover, dictate what kind of people he can associate with; to wit, other vice-ridden people. The irony in this is that, like himself, they are untrustworthy. He is, by necessity of his own choices, forced to surround himself with people whom he cannot trust.[5] The Communist totalitarian leader of Russia, Josef Stalin, was apparently in constant fear of assassination from food poisoning by his colleagues. One account claims that he regularly had three different meals served in three different ways from three different entrances at the same time, leaving any poisoners unsure of what meal to poison at any given dinner. Presumably, this ploy left the would-be assassin in fear of poisoning the wrong person.[6]

The tyrant may have supposed that by doing whatever he wishes, rather than limiting his behavior to virtuous action, he has enlarged his freedom. But, on the contrary, he has enslaved himself, blinded, as he now is, by immoral choices of action. Like virtue, vice is a fixed state of character forged by acts that, unlike virtuous acts, increasingly incline one to actions that are dehumanizing. One who is in the grip of the

---

[5] Marcia Homiak, "Moral Character" *Stanford Encyclopedia of Philosophy* (April 15, 2019). http://plato.stanford.edu/entries/moral-character/

[6] Jackie Mansky, "The True Story of the Death of Stalin." (October 10, 2017.) *Smithsonian Magazine.* *https://www.smithsonianmag.com/history/true-story-death-stalin-180965119/*

vice of lust, say, no longer sees human beings as persons of dignity, etc., but rather as objects of sexual gratification. Similarly, one in the grip of greed sees other people primarily as sources of fiscal enrichment.

All of which is why the classical moralists, Socrates, Plato, and Aristotle, saw that the primary and most serious effect of immoral behavior is the loss of rational control. And Medieval thinkers, such as Thomas Aquinas, taught that immoral acts were irrational, presupposing a theological matrix in which all actions either led to an ultimate end, God, or not. Because they saw that God was every creature's ultimate good, actions that caused one's trajectory to veer from the goal of eternity with Him were understandably seen as irrational.[7]

Some, such as Candace Vogler, fail to understand why even immoral actions, performed without any theological considerations, cannot ultimately be rational.[8]

And why not? A little parsing is called for here. To begin with, "rational" is an analogous term. If one means by it logical and consistent planning that is based on evidence, then surely immoral action can be *rational*. A lifetime of

---

[7] Shawn Floyd, "Thomas Aquinas: Moral Philosophy." *Internet Encyclopedia of Philosophy.*
htpp://www.iep.utm.edu/aq-moral/

[8] Candace Vogler, *Reasonably Vicious*. (Cambridge: Harvard University Press, 2002).

immoral behavior that has, more often than not, fulfilled one's goals can, with respect to the actions themselves, be rational, but they remain *irrational* in the sense that they frustrate the more fundamental striving for humanization. Consider Immanuel Kant's depiction of the *heteronomous* man who, from all outward appearances, is free insofar as he "chooses" what he wishes, but is, in fact, not free because his vices—greed, pride, lust—enslave him to those desires, so that he cannot "choose" other than he does.[9]

And the virtue ethics of Aristotle and Aquinas work the same way as Socratic and Kantian ethics: immoral acts are irrational because they lead to vice, a fixed state of enslavement.[10] One does not have to be aware of one's moral enslavement to be morally enslaved, a point famously dramatized by Aldous Huxley in his dystopic novel *Brave New World*: "Everyone here likes what he gets and no one likes what he can't get."

Frederico Fellini's film *La Dolce Vita*, an Italian comedy-drama produced in 1960, offers what I take to be a good example of this moral blindness/enslavement. Marcello, the film's main character, is a writer for a gossip magazine. His

---

[9] Eric Entrican Wilson and Lara Denis, "Kant and Hume on Morality" Stanford Encyclopedia of Philosophy (March 29, 2018). https://plato.stanford.edu/entries/kant-hume-morality/

[10] Garth Kemerling, "Aristotle: Ethics and Virtues." (November, 2011). http://www.philosophypages.com/hy/2s.htm

work understandably brings him into a world of morally confused and decadent people. Toward the film's end, he is driving to a party at an oceanside villa. On the way, he stops at a café for a bite to eat, and it quickly becomes clear that he and the waitress, Paola, are attracted to each other. They share warm words and inviting glances before Marcello drives to the party which is predictably populated by fitting candidates for a gossip story. The party attendees stay awake throughout the night, playing games, talking, and cavorting. As they emerge from the mansion into the morning sunlight, Fellini calls our attention to several fishermen trying to figure out how to extricate a large fish from a net. (A metaphor for the party-goers' entrapment by vices of their own making?)

Inexplicably, Paola shows up on the beach next to the villa and calls to Marcello. He sees her and hears her voice, but the wind blowing across the beach prevents him from making out what she is telling him. He turns from her and walks away. Why didn't he make an effort to walk toward her to hear what she was saying to him? Why did he just walk away instead? On the previous day, he was drawn to her, appreciative of her authenticity. But not now. Could it be that this was Fellini's way of showing that Marcello had attended one gathering of decadent people too many and had finally crossed the line, becoming decadent himself, and thus now deaf to Paola's authenticity?

Whatever message Fellini intended by his film, if he intended any at all, I believe that, *de facto,* it contains a moral tale: the freedom to choose is the freedom either to see with greater clarity what things are and what is important about other people or to become increasingly blind to what is and is not real. That's how one loses freedom. By making immoral choices, one's will increasingly rivets itself to dehumanizing objects of desire, thereby shrinking one's range of choices.

Here it would be well to point out that immoral choices can have powerful social consequences. Because not all immoral acts should be, or can be, made *illegal,* they persistently surround us with seductive examples and harmful effects. In past centuries, Vatican City, Rome, had no laws against prostitution despite the presence of prostitutes and despite the Catholic Church's teaching that prostitution is sinful. But how do we decide which *immoral* acts are to be branded as "illegal" and which should be legally allowed? The nineteenth-century philosopher, John Stuart Mill, argued that society may prevent one from acting *only* when one's action interferes with the legitimate interests of others.[11] This is a question that will not go away. Historian Richard Hofstadter writes that the founding fathers of our democracy understood that only a moral people could

---

[11] John Stuart Mill, *On Liberty,* London: Oxford University Press, p. 15

constructively possess the rights and liberties showered on them by a democracy.[12] By what right do a people kill the innocent unborn? By what right do they condone same-sex marriage?

When Mary accepted God's invitation to be the mother of Jesus, she implicitly accepted the duties and burdens of parenthood. Did she lose freedom? Yes, she gave up the freedom that comes from not having children to raise and protect. Did she also gain new freedoms? Yes, again. By accepting the invitation to be the mother of Jesus, she exercised her freedom to carry, give birth to, and raise a child. To be sure, to be childless has fewer duties than raising children, but fulfilling one's duties can bring with it a freedom of its own. To appreciate this, it is necessary to grasp the distinction between negative and positive freedom.

Negative freedom is best defined as "the absence of external restraint." Its most prominent advocate is, perhaps, John Stuart Mill. Positive freedom is more complicated, but a generalized version is "the freedom to do what is worth doing." For the classical philosophers, such as Aristotle, it was the freedom to choose to act in ways that actualized one's potencies to become more fully human; for Medievals, such as Thomas Aquinas, the desire to come closer to God energized that freedom, thereby conferring a clarity of

---

[12] Richard Hofstadter, *Anti-Intellectualism in American Life*

intellectual and spiritual vision on us, allowing us to understand more perfectly what is real and true, and therefore worth pursuing and possessing.

In terms of positive liberty, Mary's acceptance of God's invitation to be the mother of Jesus did, indeed, increase her duties, but, at the same time, it amplified her freedom by choosing to do God's will. To reiterate, our abandonment to the will of God frees us from the more mundane attachments and certainly leads us away from immoral temptations. As Father De Caussade writes in his classic work *Abandonment to Divine Providence,* even when bad things happen to us, we must realize that God allowed them to occur, knowing in His omniscience that it will be for our betterment.

In his book *The Problem of Pain,* C. S. Lewis offers a description of how people go to Hell that mirrors the classical view of how immoral choices lead to moral blindness and corresponding loss of free will. According to his account, when one dies and stands before Christ, one beholds Christ's greatness, beauty, and love, and is offered the choice of spending eternity with Him. Who could turn away from an offer like that?

Who? Anyone who has chosen a life of sin. Anyone who has lived an unrepentantly sinful life although now beholding Christ in all His glory finds it impossible to choose Him over himself. In the words of St. Paul, "For the wages of sin is death, but the gift of God is eternal life in Christ Jesus our Lord" (Romans 6:23). The sinner's Hell is eternal imprisonment within himself, the one he has repeatedly chosen over Christ. What is "Hellish" about his imprisonment is that, having rejected the absolutely perfect and loving Christ, he finds himself alone with his own finite, sinful self for eternity. Christ did not send him to Hell; he created his own Hell.[13]

Mary's "Yes" to God imposed more responsibilities on her, thereby eliminating freedoms she would otherwise have had while at the same time leading her into a world of higher, more fulfilling freedoms: carrying the God-man in her womb for nine months, giving birth to Him (presenting Him to the world), nurturing and teaching Him in preparation for His public life, the culmination of which was for Him to suffer and die for our salvation. What greater example could there be of a human being freely extending (opening) her uniqueness of self to the universality and magnificence of He who would save the world? God has a plan for each of us. If we seek to discover and follow it, we, too, shall enter a world of higher, more fulfilling freedoms. But if we choose to walk along that road, we must be willing to say, with conviction, "I am the slave of the lord."

---

[13] Peter Schakel, "Heaven and Hell as Idea and Image in C.S. Lewis." (May 7, 2010). http://www.cslewis.com/heaven-and-hell-as-idea-and-image-in-c-s-lewis/

THE 2ⁿᵈ JOYFUL MYSTERY

Mary Journeys to the Home of Elizabeth

And Mary said: "My soul proclaims the greatness of the Lord; my spirit rejoices in God my savior. For he has looked upon his handmaid's lowliness; behold, from now on will all ages call me blessed. The Mighty One has done great things for me, and holy is his name. His mercy is from age to age to those who fear him. He has shown might with his arm, dispersed the arrogant of mind and heart. He has thrown down the rulers from their thrones but lifted up the lowly. The hungry he has filled with good things; the rich he has sent away empty. He has helped Israel his servant, remembering his mercy, according to his promise to our fathers, to Abraham and to his descendants forever." (Luke 1:46-55, NAB)

At a dinner party, one of the guests compliments the hostess, saying "The food you served is delicious. You're a great cook!" And the hostess replies, "Yes, the food is delicious; and I have to agree with you: I am a great cook."

Whether the food was delicious and the hostess an exceptionally good cook, polite society regards self-praise, especially when so lavishly varnished, as excessive and uncalled for. One would have hoped that she might have instead demurely given thanks for the compliment. Mary's recitation of the *Magnificat*, which she recited upon visiting her cousin, St. Elizabeth, makes a couple of assertions that, if taken in isolation, might be seen as self-praise, but, in the context of the prayer, they are praises of gratitude to God. She states a truth: "all generations will call me blessed." Why will all generations so regard her? Because "he (God) has looked upon his handmaid's lowliness" and he (the Almighty) "has done great things for me, and holy is his name."

Clearly, Mary is not engaged in self-praise. Almighty God has asked her to be his mother. Having stated the truth, that great things have been done for her, she proceeds in the *Magnificat* to praise God not only for the great things that he has done for her but has also done and will do for all generations.

And, having acknowledged and praised God for the goodness and generosity he has bestowed on his creation, Mary proceeds to follow God's *largess* by acting with goodness and generosity toward Elizabeth.

How can we do likewise? The Corporal and Spiritual Works of Mercy are actions we can perform that extend God's compassion and mercy to those in need.

Corporal Works of Mercy

The Corporal Works of Mercy are these kinds of acts by which we help our neighbors with their material and physical needs.

feed the hungry
shelter the homeless
clothe the naked
visit the sick and the imprisoned
bury the dead
give alms to the poor

Spiritual Works of Mercy

The Spiritual Works of Mercy are acts of compassion, as listed below, by which we help our neighbors with their emotional and spiritual needs.

instruct
advise
console
comfort
forgive
bear wrongs patiently

Who is my neighbor? Christ's tale of the *Good Samaritan* tells us that everyone in need, whom we are in a position to help, is our neighbor. But, as in all choices, the virtue of prudence dictates. For example, knowing whether we *can* help, whether we *should* help, and *how* to help can be complicated and even daunting. Permit me to share one of my own experiences with you.

I was strolling down the main street in Toronto on a warm Friday evening about 50 years ago; it was about 10 PM. A couple of blocks ahead of me, I saw a city bus and several cars stopped in the street; I could see that the bus driver and passengers were on the bus, and a crowd of people were standing on the sidewalks looking at something going on. When I got there, I saw what drew their attention. A man, somewhere in his 20s, was beating up a woman of about the same age. I saw him knock her down and after she got to her feet, it looked, from where I was standing, that he tried to kick her in the stomach. Nobody was doing anything but watching. I was telling myself that I had to do something to help her, when a muscular man with a shaved head and wearing a tank top T shirt (funny, the things you remember) charged out of the tavern across the street from us and engaged the attacker, knocking him to the ground. The battered woman covered her abuser protectively with her own body before helping him to his feet. I don't recall whether she said anything to her rescuer; I do remember her and her "boyfriend" walking away from the crowd of observers, and if memory serves me, he then took the opportunity to profess his "devotion" to her, proclaiming, "I love you, baby!" The sight and sound of this was like a perverse, surreal interpretation of the ending of the first act of Puccini's opera, *La Boheme,* with Rodolfo and Mimi serenading each other as they strolled away from their friends. How often he beat her up with the two of them then

27

walking off, arm in arm, I have no idea. Had I attempted to protect her, he might well have beaten me up and then topped off his fistic behavior with his apparently usual declaration of love: the *Knuckle Serenade.*

Nevertheless, would I have called the police or enlisted one or two other males to help me restrain her mauler? But for the life of me, I can't recall whether these options even entered my mind, although under the circumstances they're so obviously the things to do. I didn't even *think* it odd that nobody called the police. About helping her, the most important help she needed was on the psychiatrist's couch.

Given that the injunction to help our neighbor *in need* presupposes that we are *morally* free to help and that we do not have other important obligations that helping our neighbor in a particular instance would jeopardize. Mary's acceptance to bear the baby Jesus was not jeopardized by her decision to journey to her cousin, St. Elizabeth, who, now pregnant in her advanced years, was most likely in need of help. Mary stayed, helping Elizabeth for three months. True, although before Mary's visit an angel assured Joseph that Mary's pregnancy was the act of the Holy Spirit, it would be no exaggeration to say that Mary still had a lot on her mind, what with the thought of the forthcoming birth of Jesus. Nevertheless, her concern for her cousin's welfare was important to her, so she journeyed to her home to help her despite concerns of her own.

Mary's visit to her cousin was an occasion for helping her in need with the Corporal and Spiritual works of Mercy. There are, to be sure, levels of sacrifice for the benefit of others. Giving up one's life for another is the greatest sacrifice: "Greater love has no man than giving his life for another." The crowning example of this is, of course, Christ's choice to suffer and die for us. In extreme cases, charity dominates. Consider, for example, how Francisco Suarez, the Spanish Jesuit theologian and philosopher (1548-1617), addressed the following challenge to natural law ethics: If two people fall overboard at sea and only one life preserver is available, which one of them has the right to it? Suarez replies that the rule of justice does not apply to the case; charity takes over: one of them offers the life preserver to the other, ideally to the one whose survival is more important, such as a man or woman with a young family to raise or a leader of a country whose people need his political skill and commitment to the common good.

How about a less dramatic example? At a restaurant luncheon, a group of people are engaged in what might be called "idle chit-chat" until one of them introduces the subject of her mother-in-law, whom she dislikes because of her meddlesome presence in her marriage. Her husband quickly joins in the conversation and is as equally critical of his mother as is his wife. In no time, their comments deteriorate into a pastiche of jokes about her shortcomings. A young woman in the group, who had been silent until then, said to the couple, "Why are you talking that way about her? Instead of making fun of her, why don't you discuss how to help her be a better person?"

Sometimes, helping our neighbor in need means keeping our mouths shut. Consider: Jones and Smith hold sharply divided political views, and Smith has publicly stated on several occasions that Jones has " the IQ of a fruit fly." At the annual company Christmas party, a former co-worker of Smith tells Jones that, contrary to Smith's claim that he was released from the U. S. Army during the Korean War to help his family through its financial hardship, Smith was given a *Bad Conduct Discharge* for assault and battery on another soldier. Understandably, Jones is powerfully tempted to publicize Smith's blemished past. I would argue that *gratuitously* doing so would be *destructive* rather than *constructive* –to Smith's marriage and three children—and therefore morally unjustifiable. Thus, Jones would help Smith—his fellow human being and thus his *neighbor*—by remaining silent on that matter.

And what about people who have a professional obligation to teach the truth: bishops, priests, Catholic school teachers, and university professors? Does their conspicuous silence on "touchy" but important topics— contraception, same-sex marriage, abortion, secularism, and transsexuality, etc.—help their neighbors, and members of their flock in need? The answer is "No"; for it leaves the media as the primary teacher of the public.

And how about helping our neighbor when they are ignorant, or at least uncertain, of their need? When you address an audience on a controversial topic, especially a large audience, you never know who and how many you will reach. Consider the following email I received from a former student of mine at the university.

"Dear Professor Dennehy,

I just wanted to thank you for your class this semester and what you taught us about abortion. I can't help but feel as if God had led me to your class.

I came in pessimistic and cynical about the 'pro-life' view and left completely confused and dare I say, changed.

Shortly after that class, I found out I'm pregnant and as I contemplated keeping this baby or getting an abortion, I remembered I saved all the articles you gave us. I read through all of them more intensely than ever and decided that as a moral being, I could not terminate this human life inside of me. Both my now husband and I made the decision to keep our baby boy, and I can't thank you enough. It is a decision we made with peace and contentedness. We are happier than ever.

Attached is his latest ultrasound picture. We are 7 months along and naming him ….. Again, thank you for changing my/our views to make room for this blessing!

Best Regards,

[Signed…….]"

Yes, you never know how many members of your audience you've managed to reach, but they have to hear the right message, in this case about the intrinsic value of unborn human life. Otherwise, they may remain content with the false view advocated by the anti-life side.

When we broach topics about helping our neighbor, it's understandable that *individuals* and *their families* come to mind: the laborer down the street whose sudden fatal heart attack left his wife and four children without any means of support or the homeless encamped in the city park.

But we must not forget to include in our picture of the poor and homeless the impoverished nations of the world. In March of 1967, St. Pope Paul VI presented his encyclical, "On the Development of Nations" (*Populorum Progressio*). This document addressed the growing gap between rich and poor nations. One of his main objections was the formulation of that disparity in terms of rapid growth in world population rather than the failure of the rich nations to come to the aid of the impoverished nations. (See James Schall, S. J., *Human Dignity and Human Numbers,* St Pauls, Alba House Publishers, 1971.)

A popular song of the 1950s, sung by Kitty Kallen, celebrates a principle that transcends the song's *romantic* context: most of the time, helping our neighbor in need doesn't require Herculean exertion:

Blow me a kiss from across the room
Say I look nice when I'm not
Touch my hair as you pass my chair
Little things mean a lot
Give me your arm as we cross the street
Call me at six on the dot
A line a day when you're far away
Little things mean a lot
Don't have to buy me diamonds and pearls
Champagne, sables or such
I never cared much for diamonds and pearls
Cause honestly honey, they just cost money
Give me your hand when I've lost the way
Give me your shoulder to cry on
Whether the day is bright or gray
Give me your heart to rely on
Send me the warmth of a secret smile
To show me you haven't forgot
For always and ever, now and forever
    Little things mean a lot
    (Kitty Kallen, *Metrolyrics*)

At all events, the *Corporal and Spiritual Works of Mercy,* enumerated by Christ in the Gospel, along with His parable of the *Good Samaritan,* are always there to guide us in helping those in need.

THE 3RD JOYFUL MYSTERY

The Birth of Christ

"EVERY CHILD A WANTED CHILD"

This motto frequently appears on the rear bumper of automobiles. Public sentiment agrees with its proclamation. But caution is needed, for that bumper sticker can have a sinister purpose. Of course, every child *should* be wanted, but not every child *is* wanted. What to do about unwanted children? Some supporters of the bumper sticker have an answer: abort them. Here's a case of economics absorbing ethics. How? By reducing unborn human beings to the status of saleable products. Economists call it *valorization*: a product's value depends on the law of supply and demand. If, for example, the demand for Volkswagen automobiles exceeds the supply of available Volkswagen automobiles, the cost of the cars rises; if the supply of available Volkswagens exceeds the number of people who wish to buy them, then the cost of the cars decreases.

Valorization, it is clear, acknowledges no value in products for which there is no demand because the value ascribed to products is *extrinsic* rather than *intrinsic*. The product's value does not originate in the product itself but in people's desire to acquire it. In contrast, a human being's value—even an unborn human being—does not depend on its being wanted since its value is *intrinsic*: human beings are valuable in themselves because of *who they are*.

It is appropriate to mention, at this early part of the essay, that depictions of Mary by herself are incomplete. They do, to be sure, inspire devotion to the Mother of God, but the absence of the child Jesus from the depictions must not lead us to forget or even minimize her significance as the *Mother of God*.

Why did God choose to be born of a woman rather than redeeming us directly and immediately without leaving Heaven or by coming from Heaven as a thirty-year-old, so He could begin His public life right away? Why, instead, did He choose the entire human experience: *in utero* conception and gestation, infancy, adolescence, and adulthood? I haven't checked this out, but I surmise that His reason for choosing the longer, more scenic route, was to show how great His love for us is by becoming *our brother*: the infinite being, God Almighty, was also totally a human being—not a Divine Being *using* a human body, but one single being, totally Divine and totally human, offering on the cross a rich existence of *lived human experiences*, experiences that require living in and through the major stages of human development. In other words, the life that Christ gave up for us was not a life of symbolic gestures or bloodless concepts. Although Christ is God and therefore transcends creation, He expresses His infinite love for us by sharing our human experiences. Again: "He became like us in all things except sin."

Christ was born in a stable and placed in a manger. Apparently, Mary and Joseph did not have high end medical coverage. Although He is God, Christ chose also to be a human being. It is beyond our powers of understanding to grasp how Christ could, at once, be both God and man: there He was, lying in the manger, as helpless and vulnerable as any newborn. Did Mary know that her baby was God? I wonder if she didn't know it then because even twelve years later when she and Joseph found Jesus in the temple, lecturing to adults learned in scripture, she asked:

"Son, why have you done this to us? Your father and I have been looking for you with great anxiety." And he said to them, "Why were you looking for me? Did you not know that I must be in my Father's house?" But they did not understand what he said to them." (Luke 2: 48-50 NAB)

If she knew or even suspected her Son's Divinity, would she have asked herself such a question? Years later, at the wedding feast in Cana, Christ was clearly not ready to start His public life when Mary urged Him to help the wedding couple out of their wine shortage, as He replied, "Woman, how does your concern affect me? My hour has not yet come" (John 2:4 NAB). She nevertheless said to the head of catering, "Do whatever he tells you" (John 2:5 NAB). Would she have taken that approach had she known her Son was God? Would she have urged Him to start His public life? Yes.

Why "Yes"? To my way of thinking, Christ was born into an authentic family, which is to say that Joseph wasn't just *acting* as a father, neither was Mary just *acting* as a mother nor was Christ just *acting* as a human son. And Scripture tells us that the wedding guests weren't *pretending* that Christ made wine from water; on the contrary, it was *real wine*, and *very good wine*, at that. If the Holy Family was a genuine family—as I believe it was—both Mary and Joseph must have had a parent's natural and spontaneous authority over their Son, Jesus, and He, in turn, must have had a natural and spontaneous obedience toward His parents. Do those considerations add up to claiming that they had a natural right to expect obedience from Jesus, so that, even though Mary and Joseph knew Jesus was God, when Mary made clear that she wanted Her Son to provide more wine for the Cana wedding feast, He made more wine? And what, in the first place, are we to say about the fact that she was confident that He could produce more wine for the feast? Are we to suppose that Mary believed that He possessed divine powers to change water into wine and therefore *knew* that her son, Jesus, was God?

But, at all events, Christ was both God and man in a single substance and self with a real father and a real mother, both of whom He needed for love and proper development.

All in all, this adds up to the truth that Mary's importance to Christ's life is that she is the *Theotokos, of whom it is said in the Greek Orthodox Church, "the love poured into the Theotokos* to enable her to love so fully in her turn."

All of which is to say that paintings and other depictions of Mary with the baby Jesus have a completeness that cannot be matched by depictions of Mary alone. To repeat, this, to be sure, is not to say that depictions of Mary alone express a falsehood, for praying to Mary and asking her to intercede on our behalf is laudable and effective. Surely, Christ came to her frequently asking for help in various matters. And prayer to Mary leads us to Christ. After all, she brought Christ into the world with her "Yes" to the angel Gabriel: "Behold, I am the *slave girl* of the Lord."

And still another question: Does Herod's order to his soldiers to kill all children under two years of age connect with today's pro-abortion movement? If there is a connection, it doesn't seem to be a strong one. Herod gave the order because he feared that one of the babies born during the past two years of his reign was slated to replace him as Roman client king of Judea. The massacre of those innocents was his way of eliminating the unwelcome possibility of losing his kingship. What, exactly, is the connection with today's legalized abortion practice? Apparently, not much unless one would be satisfied with the foggy connection that both seem to be found under the heading of *convenience:* Whereas Herod murdered children to protect his client kingship, perhaps in the belief that he had a right to be King of Judea, people today kill the unborn in the belief that they have a right to sex without pregnancy. Contraception fosters this belief. Admittedly, contraception differs from abortion since, while induced abortion directly kills unborn human beings, contraception only prevents the *possibility* of conception. Sometimes, though, it is also abortifacient. In his encyclical *The Gospel of Life*, Pope St. John Paul II unveiled the connection between contraception and abortion: the contraceptive mentality believes that one has a right to sex without conceiving human life; so, in the event of an unwanted pregnancy, abortion is justified as the means of protecting that right.[14] Herod's mass killing of children under two years of age was more brutal than today's "medically clean" abortions. But wait! The New York State Legislators have recently legalized killing a human fetus with a beating heart who has survived abortion. We're on the way to catching up with King Herod on more brutal ways to kill children!

The horror of *directly killing innocent children* is in the *act of directly killing* them not in the social status of the agent who kills them: The educated physician who directly expels a nonviable fetus from a woman's uterus acts every bit as

---

[14] *The Gospel of Life* (Evangelium Vitae, March 25, 1995) Pope John Paul II. (Boston, MA: Pauline Books & Media), pp. 27-29.

brutally as the uneducated Judean soldier who slashed a baby's throat with a sword. Again, the horror of *directly killing innocent children* is in the *act of directly killing them*, not in the means used to kill them: Killing babies with a sword is, to be sure, a ghastly deed; but the direct killing of unborn humans by means of surgical scissors or toxins is, despite its sterile setting, no less ghastly.

Supporters of legalized abortion object to this line of argument by calling attention to the U. S. Supreme Court's *Roe v. Wade* decision in 1973. The Court ruled that the *Right to Privacy* is a Constitutionally protected right and that it implies a woman's right to demand an abortion. Apparently, the judges who voted for the right to abortion failed to see that they thereby vaporized the foundation of all rights.

How? Because the right to life is the primary right. All other rights presuppose it. Any society that no longer commits itself to defending the right to life has no absolute rationale for defending any other right: freedom of speech, of worship, of peaceful public assembly, including any "right to privacy." If the right to life is a negotiable commodity, then, by parity of reason, so must all other rights be negotiable commodities; since if innocent human beings can legally directly be killed, then what's to stop the government from "justifiably" muzzling free speech, or prohibiting religious worship or peaceful public assembly?

What about the pro-abortion claim that the fetus is not a human being, or at least not a person, and thus not a subject of rights? The question of when human life begins is, as Mortimer Adler stated, a "mixed question" because, in addition to scientific knowledge, philosophical knowledge is also required, but the scientific knowledge is primary. First of all, mammalian reproduction is characterized by *continuity of nature.* When the male sperm penetrates the female ovum, each is transmuted: whereas before their interaction, the sperm had the genotype of every cell in the male's body and the ovum had the genotype of every cell in the female's body, the genotype of both sperm and ovum is changed as the being that is produced from the interaction, the *zygote,* has a genotype that is different from both the male's and the female's genotypes. Thus, it cannot legitimately be called a part of the female's body. The bodily organs of the mother work for the survival and health of her body, but, during pregnancy those same organs also work for the survival, health, and development of the newly created being, as it passes through its stages of embryo, fetus, and infant.

Some pro-abortionists argue that the fetus is *de facto* part of the woman's body because its survival depends on the nourishment and protection it gets from her and thus bestows on her the rights of the same disposition that she has over her body parts. But the error of this argument is its supposition that dependency confers rights of disposal. A small child depends on its parents for shelter, protection, guidance, and feeding, etc., and could scarcely be counted on to survive if turned out into the streets on its own. Who would say that this dependency on adults confers on them the right to kill or maim their child? Granted, the child has already been born and thus no longer has the intimate and direct dependence on the mother's bodily functions that it required during its prenatal stage of life. But even *in utero,* its genotype differed from its mother's, differed from every cell in her body. The embryo is no more *a part* of the mother's body before birth than it is after birth. *Dependency* does not necessarily mean *absolute ownership.*

Moreover, we have no evidence where two members of the same species produce a being of a different species. Yes, a horse and a donkey, a lion and a leopard, can produce offspring, but such offspring are categorized as *hybrids* instead of *species* because they cannot reproduce. The human fetus is the product of a human mother and a human father; if it's not a human being, what is it?

From the philosophical standpoint, some pro-abortionists argue that the fetus is a legitimate human being from the get-go, but is human only *genetically,* not *morally.* They argue that to be a human being in the *moral* sense, a human being must be a *person* and only persons qualify as subjects of rights. Pro-abortionist and feminist, the late Mary Ann Warren, with whom I had the pleasure of publicly debating abortion on three or four occasions, regarded five traits as central to the concept of personhood:

(1) consciousness (of objects and events external and/or internal to the being), and in particular the capacity to feel pain;

(2) reasoning (the *developed* capacity to solve new and relatively complex problems);

(3) self-motivated activity (activity which is relatively independent of either genetic or direct external control);

(4) the capacity to communicate, by whatever means, messages of an indefinite variety of types, that is not just with an indefinite number of possible contents, but on indefinitely many possible topics;

(5) the presence of self-concepts, and self-awareness, either individual or racial, or both.[15]

Warren speculated that "(1) and (2) alone might be sufficient conditions for personhood and more probably (1)–(3) are sufficient. No one of the five may be sufficient to be a person, though (1)-(3) seem to be necessary conditions for it." At all events, she insists that no being which satisfies none of the criteria is a person. But Stephan Schwarz correctly notes that Warren's functionalism fails to accom-

---

[15] Mary Ann Warren, "On the Moral and Legal Status of Abortion." Biomedical Ethics. 4th ed. T.A. Mappes and D. DeGrazia, eds. (New York: McGraw-Hill, Inc. 1996), pp. 434-440. https://spot.colorado.edu/~norcross/Ab3.pdf

modate the reality that one can *be a person* without *functioning* as a person. [16]

Because the fetus is a human being and thus a member of the human species, he or she is *by nature* a rational being and thus a *person*. Life in the womb is a time of fundamental organic development, and rationality emerges when the relevant organic support has unfolded. If the embryo were not a person, it would not have the *capacity* to develop the rational functions of a person. [17]

Back to the Holy Family. Mary and Joseph were able to get out of Dodge with Jesus, thanks to an angel warning them that their Son's life was in immediate and grave danger. Thereby hangs a tale. Above, I said that as He lay in the manger, Jesus, despite His Divinity, looked as helpless and vulnerable as any other infant. Yet, He had a future ahead of Him that was infinitely noble and glorious for all its love and generosity. All babies have futures; God has a plan for each of us. When we unjustly kill children—or adults, for that matter—we disrupt God's plan for them.

A case in point is the Civil Rights leader, Jesse Jackson. A Baptist Minister, he founded *Operation Push* to aid the poor

---

[16] Steven Schwarz, *The Moral Question of Abortion*. (Chicago: University of Loyola Press, 1990).

[17] Dianne N. Irving, "When do Human Beings Begin? 'Scientific Myths and Scientific Facts'"
http://www.princeton.edu/~prolife/articles/wdhbb.html

and provide educational opportunities for disadvantaged children, in addition to speaking out against the morally harmful influence of much popular music and entertainment on our youth. In the January, 1979, edition of the *National Right to Life News,* he wrote an article against abortion. Therein, the Rev. Jackson met, head on, all the major arguments for abortion: the fetus is not a human being, a woman has the right to privacy, unborn babies faced with mental, physical, or socio-economic disadvantages are better off not being born, and so forth.

What made his anti-abortion argument compelling was that he prefaced it with the revelation that he himself was illegitimate and that his mother was pressured to abort him. Had she submitted, there would not have been any Jesse Jackson and having been robbed of his future, he would not have lived to perform all the above good works. Don Marquis' essay "Why Abortion is Immoral" advances the argument that what makes abortion of fetuses immoral is that it deprives them of "a future like ours."[18] All babies, as they lay in the crib, look as they are: helpless and vulnerable. We cannot be sure how any of them will turn out. Maybe the child, in the womb of the prostitute or drug addict will also become a prostitute or drug addict or, worse yet, a violent criminal. But if we abort her baby, we won't ever know

---

[18] Don Marquis, "Why Abortion is Immoral." *Journal of Philosophy*, April, 1989.

because death destroys all possibilities. When Jessie Jackson threw his hat into the ring for the 1984 Democratic Presidential candidacy, he announced his about-face change of position on abortion. He had become prochoice. So much for the evil of abortion!

About the future, we can never be sure; we can only hope and pray. As of 2021, over 60 million legal abortions have been performed in the United States since the U.S. Supreme Court rendered the Roe v. Wade decision in 1973. That means that since then legal abortion in the United States has taken more lives than we lost in the total number killed in the Revolutionary War, the Civil War (both North and South), World War I, World War II, the Korean war, the Vietnam war, and the first Gulf War.[19] We don't know how many innocents King Herod slaughtered, but that number of deaths is beyond doubt dwarfed by the number of innocents slaughtered by Roe v. Wade.

Christ chose to be born of a woman. In what follows, I beg the reader's indulgence as I quote at length from my introduction to the book, *Christian Married Love*.[20]

---

[19] Vasu Murti, *The Liberal Case Against Abortion*, Mt. Laurel, N.J., Rage Media, 2006.

[20] Christian Married Love, Edited and with an Introduction by Raymond Dennehy, San Francisco: Ignatius Press, 1981; Rpt 2018, pp. 10-12.

"It is impossible to understand the significance that the Western World attaches to the human sex act apart from the context of the Judeo-Christian tradition. The dignity that this tradition sees in human sexuality has its explanation in the fact that it is regarded as the creaturely analogue of God's creative power. Having made us in His own image and likeness, He invites us to participate in His providence. In the sex act, we cooperate with Him in the creation of new human life. In doing so, He also calls upon us to take responsibility for that life. Thus, the sex act is a participation in God's Fatherly concern for his creatures, as well as in His creative power, because parental love is at once protective and respectful of the child's freedom and integrity. Like God's love for us, then, parental love risks rejection, misunderstanding, and even ridicule. As parents, we remain vulnerable at the hands of both the beloved and the world. Yet, insofar as our sex act remains open to procreation, we freely accept that risk. But the willingness to accept risk is understandable in terms of the principle, *The good is diffusive.* Just as God, who is supremely good, freely created the world in generosity and love for the creatures He would bring into existence, so the Judeo-Christian tradition views the sex act as an expression of love and generosity.

"It is at this point that the Church's insistence on the moral impossibility of separating the *unitive* and *procreative* aspects of the sex act derives its intelligibility. For this is the act in which a man and woman express their mutual love and, in so doing, donate themselves to each other in such a way as to procreate another human being. Because love is by its nature creative, the expression of their love for each other, which the act makes possible in a unique way, is inextricably tied to that act's openness to procreation. Thus, as Bishop Cahal Daly observes, to say that in marriage a man and a woman become two in one flesh is not simply to speak metaphorically; it is to state a literal truth. Their love is incarnated in the child. Even from a purely biological standpoint, the child gets twenty-three chromosomes from each parent. Thus, although the child is a person and accordingly in his or her uniqueness is more than the sum of parental contributions, it is nevertheless true to say that in an important sense that child gets his or her being from his parents. Since the child is the embodiment of their love for each other and since this love is a donating of self, each to the other, we may fairly say that it is in him or her that they actually become two in one flesh. Indeed, as Daly further observes, this expression of their love will endure forever because the child is a person and, as such, is destined by God to live for eternity. This becoming "two in one flesh" is also verified on the dynamic level of day-to-day family relations. It is impossible to assess the husband's and wife's love for each other apart from their love for the child, while in turn their love for him or her cannot properly be assessed apart from their love for each other."

Daly writes, "It is in the dogma of the Trinity, however, that we find the highest and most influential model for the sexual union between man and woman. Only in the Trinity is there love so perfect that the Lovers' communion ---their respective donation of selves --- is so perfect that the result is perfect unity, one God; and yet, because donation is an act that can be performed only by persons, their love preserves the uniqueness of the three persons, Father, Son, and Holy Spirit. Because love is fruitful and because the love between the Father and the Son is a perfect love, it is the most perfectly fruitful of all love: its issue is the Holy Spirit. Thus modeled, as it is after the Holy Trinity, the conception of love between man and woman, as it has permeated the West and its institutions, is a love that is unitive without destroying the unique selfhood of each, and is also creative --- it results in a new human person. And just as the love between the Father and the Son could not exist apart from the issuing of the Holy Spirit, so the unitive and procreative aspects of human love cannot be separated. Indeed, just as the Divine love is essentially and thus eternally Trinitarian, so is the love among man, woman, and offspring; for, as noted above, one cannot properly understand the love between man and woman apart from their love for their child and vice versa. In this mutual expression of a love that in its super-abundance overflows to create a new person, both the man and the woman enjoy a self-fulfillment that they could not otherwise enjoy; for their growth in love for each other and their personal growth are uniquely dependent on the love and care they have for their child.[21]

"Now if the three attributes of the human sex act – unity, creativity, and self-fulfillment – owe their affirmation and emphasis to the doctrines of theology and the general cultural impact of religion, then the emergence of secularism threatens to erase them from modern man's perception of that act. For the widespread practice of contraception, along with the apologies for it, presuppose an entirely different model from the Divine. The results, which are becoming increasingly evident, are marital disintegration, sterility, and unhappiness." Mary Eberstadt's recent book, *Adam and Eve After the Pill* presents an eye-opening account of how the current growth of the contraceptive mentality undermines marriage and respect for women.[22]

A final point: The attempt to justify homosexuality as a normal expression of sexual attraction and love directly follows from the justification for contraception. For if sex can formally be separated from the openness to procreation, as contraception does, then it is impossible to condemn any form of sexual activity that is freely entered into by adults and that does not injure the participants. The consequences

---

[21] Cahal Daly, *Morals, Law, and Life.* (Chicago, Dublin, London: Scepter Books, 1962).

[22] Mary Eberstadt, *Adam and Eve After the Pill.* (San Francisco: Ignatius Press, 2012).

of socially legitimized homosexual behavior, such as what was done in *Obergefell v. Hodges,* 576 U.S. 644 (2015), can only result in disaster. *Genesis tells us that it is not good for man to be alone and thus God created a partner for Adam, the woman, Eve,* not another Adam. And Aristotle stated that the relationship between *man and woman* is the basis for the constitution of the city-state. Men and women are importantly different; each has what the other lacks but needs. Two men together cannot produce what a man and woman together can produce besides children, nor can two women.

That the Catholic Church does not condemn sex between married couples for whom sterility prevents procreation or between couples using *Natural Family Planning* (NFP), does not, as some would have us believe, justify a married couple's use of contraception or homosexual relationships. Here, I must again beg the reader's indulgence as I quote at length from my article, "Contraception and Homosexuality."

"A common objection to Natural Family Planning is that it is hypocritical because its goal is identical to that of contraception – sex without pregnancy. But the two forms of birth control are worlds apart. The charge of hypocrisy rests on at least two false assumptions. The first is that the Catholic Church's condemnation supposes that it is evil to desire sex without babies. But surely there is nothing wrong with that desire. Nature does not intend every act of sexual intercourse to result in pregnancy since a woman is fertile for only a few days a month while the sex drive expresses itself throughout the month. The charge of hypocrisy also implies a failure to distinguish between a desire and the *means of realizing the desire*. In using NFP, the couple do nothing to obstruct the possibility of conception in that particular act; on the contrary, they remain open to the production of new human life. In fact, it would be wrong to think of NFP simply as a way of avoiding children since many couples practice it to pinpoint when the woman is ovulating as a way of increasing their chances of conceiving a child. NFP does not formally separate sex from procreation."[23]

About fifty years ago or so a movement started in America with the motto, "Keep Christ in Christmas." We hardly hear that anymore and "Merry Christmas" is now a politically incorrect felicitation and is, with increasing frequency, replaced with "Happy Holidays," while the "Christmas Season" is replaced by the "Holiday Season." And where's the Christ child? Can His now empty crib serve as a metaphor for the empty cribs in society, thanks to the contraceptive revolution?

Discussion of transgenderism here? It's a very, very disturbing movement, and I wonder if clerics realize that?

---

[23] California Association of Natural Family Planning News, Summer, 2007.

God told Adam, "It is not good for man to be alone." Thus, He created woman, created her from Adam's rib. What's the significance of that?

Embryology tells us that gender is determined at the very moment when the sperm from the male penetrates and interacts with the ovum of the female. At that moment, the conceptus has two genes, either an X gene and a Y gene or two X genes. From that moment, its genotype is then, and forever, male or female. The male has an X chromosome and a Y chromosome while the female has two X chromosomes. The *Biology Dictionary* defines the genotype of an organism "as the chemical composition of its DNA, which gives rise to the phenotype, or observable traits of an organism."

Advocates of transsexuality, gender feminists are an example, claim that, although sexual differences between men and women are real, gender is a *social construct,* like the rules of grammar. For example, "table" in Spanish, *la mesa,* is feminine, but in German, it's masculine, *der Tisch;* hence, while the *transgender movement* cannot plausibly deny the reality of sexual difference between men and women (they *do* try!), since that is established from the moment of conception when sperm and ovum interact, each with the other, to produce an XX or XY genotype, they feel free to deny the ontological/biological and *pre-social* reality of maleness and femaleness.

Is the distinction between man and woman important, in fact, irreplaceable? God told Adam, "It is not good for man to be alone. I will make a suitable partner for him. (*Genesis 2,18*) By creating a female human being, God was sending a message: men and women need each other. As stated above, women lack but need what men have, and men lack but need what women have. As a popular song of past decades puts it, "Man, O' man is for the woman made and the woman is made for man." From another song: "But there's nothing worse in the universe than a woman without a man." And here's a title from a book that discusses the significance and importance of the difference between the sexes: *Men Are from Mars, Women Are from Venus.* Catchy title, no?[24]

So, what happens to human life and culture if a society buys into the view that human beings are either pure spirits somehow encased in male or female bodies that have no relation to their true selves or, if materialists, believe that they are trapped and frustrated by a gender label society has imposed on them that collides with their self-image?

God's words to Adam imply that his male gender was an integral part of him and that Eve's female gender was an integral part of her. Hence, as noted above, in his lectures on the Human Person, Pope St. John Paul II taught that our bodies are just as much a part of our personhood as our souls. This view harks back to Thomas Aquinas' commentary on Aristotle's treatise on the soul. Thomas

---

[24] John Gray, Ph.D. *Men Are from Mars, Women Are from Venus* (New York: Harper Collins Publishers, 1992).

underscores the words "potentially alive." The soul is not, he tells us, united to a living body; it is united to matter, and a living body is the consequence of such a union. Otherwise, it would be a case of joining two substances. But then there could only result an *accidental* union.[25]

From this, we can infer that the reality of a given man is contingent on the composite of matter and form. In other words, the human body is not a mere encasement of the soul, but rather its material expression.

Consider, for example, the human hand. It is an inferior striking weapon in comparison to the Grizzly Bear's fearsome paw; an inferior prehensile tool in comparison to the gigantic gripping strength of the Orangutan. But in its versatility and sensitivity, it is quite superior to the "tools" of brute animals. Observe the hands of a pianist as he plays a Bach *Fugue* or a Chopin *Etude*. Note the delicacy and coloring of intellectual and emotional expression of which they are capable as they move over the keyboard. The human hand can translate abstract ideas into concrete and material forms of expression. It is an instrument whose structure and versatility of operation follow from its belonging to a rational being. It is more versatile than prodigious because it is an

---

[25] *Commentary of St. Thomas Aquinas on Aristotle's Treatise on the Soul.* Trans. by R.A. Kocourek. https://archive.org/details/CommentaryOfSt.ThomasAquinasOn AristotlesTreatiseOnTheSoul.Tanslated

instrument of intellectual expression in the material realm. Because the intellect is universal in its capacity for knowing and creating, the instrument of its concrete expression, the hand must possess something of the same universality. This is what it means to say that human beings are *rational animals.* We are not rationality juxtaposed to animality, but rather we are beings in which rationality permeates and dominates animality. Hence, to repeat St. John Paul II's words, "our bodies are just as much our personhood as our souls."

If Christ were not both God and man but instead God tricked out in human features, His suffering and death would have been a sham. If Mary had not really been impregnated by the Holy Spirit and given birth to God, the Son, who was like us in all things except sin, then His Incarnation, suffering and death, the Holy Family itself, would have been Kabuki Theater.

But our Redeemer was not hiding behind a mask. Before ascending into Heaven, He reassured the Apostles and surely His mother, Mary, that He had their backs, and we have every confidence that He has our backs as well. The point of it all must not be forgotten or trivialized and is worth repeating: Our bodies are just as much our personhood as our souls. Hence, Jesus is both divine and human, shedding real blood, *His blood,* suffering real pain, *His pain,* and dying a real death, *His death.* Today's Gnostics and Neo-Gnostics deny the meaning and value of their respective maleness and femaleness, thereby implicitly embracing fantasies that invite bodily experimentation that is, in fact, bodily mutilation and that, along with contraception and abortion, paves the road to the end of democracy.

THE 4TH JOYFUL MYSTERY

Mary and Joseph Present the Child Jesus in the Temple

For many years, I had no enthusiasm for meditating on this Mystery until its Incarnational significance confronted me. An online guide for praying the Rosary[26] cites the concept of *Obedience* as the "fruit of meditation" on this Mystery and draws from a popular online encyclopedia site, Wikipedia.org, to emphasize the difference between *obedience* and *compliance:* in Obedience, human behavior, is a form of "social influence in which a person yields to explicit instructions or orders from an authority figure."[27] "Obedience is generally distinguished from *compliance*, which is behavior influenced by peers, and from *conformity*, which is behavior intended to match that of the majority."[28]

Christ, the God-man, enters the world of human affairs, laws, and traditions, presenting God's love ever more fully to the world. The Hypostatic Union tells us that God, by becoming human, chose to be *our brother*, "like us in all things except sin." Mary and Joseph brought Him to the

---

[26] Rosarymeds.com. https://www.rosarymeds.com/rosary-basics/

[27] Andrew Colman, "Obedience." *A Dictionary of Psychology.* (Oxford, NY: Oxford University Press, 2009).

[28] "Obedience (Human Behavior), Wikipedia.org, https://en.wikipedia.org/wiki/Obedience_(human_behavior)

temple to be consecrated to God, a commitment that involved circumcision. Living in the world means living according to laws, traditions, dangers, and the wishes of others. This is true of Christ in all the Rosary's mysteries that portray Him. To borrow an aphorism from the philosopher, Yves R. Simon, "To exist is not enough; *il faut agir* [it is necessary to act]."[29] Christ lived His thirty-three years of life on earth to the hilt. We can safely say that while He refrained from using vulgar language, telling off-color jokes, or engaging in harmful or even unflattering gossip about others, Christ was far from being a passive observer merely waiting for His time to suffer and die. Wherever He went, He made a difference. Of course, speech is not the only way of influencing others.

For example, when I was in the Navy, the ports of call our ship visited in Asia each year offered many taverns and brothels for the sailors. It was in that environment that I discovered the power of obedience in the humble manner of an unmarried shipmate who would visit the taverns, have a drink or two, and even dance with the bar girls, but would never have sex with the prostitutes. He was a Christian who unobtrusively read his Bible every day; never did I hear him utter a profanity, and never to my knowledge, did he say

---

[29] Anthony O. Simon (Editor), *Acquaintance with the Absolute.* (New York: Fordham University Press, 1998), p. 19.

anything to the other sailors, including the married ones, about their sexual behavior with the "ladies of the evening"; on the contrary, he was always pleasant and helpful. And, to boot, his performance as a sailor was outstanding. What became clear was that his silence and humility spoke loud and pointedly to his fellow sailors so they couldn't resist joking about his chastity. Why? Because, to use another image, his chastity and *silent* presence were, in effect, a mirror to them of their infidelities. This taught me that example, especially when fueled by obedience, as a commitment, inspires it, and however humble and quiet, does not go unnoticed. We cannot tell how what we might consider our daily acts and words, however humble, influence others.

Mary and Joseph were humble as they followed Jewish law by going to the temple to consecrate their son, Jesus, to God. By word and deed, parents can provide their children with a moral and religious context for their lives, thereby teaching them *to put God first,* etc. Of course, there's no telling for sure how beginnings, though humdrum, will end up. Consider, for example, Adolf Hitler (Adolf Schicklgruber, 1889-1945), who was baptized a Catholic in Austria only to become a monstrous tyrant, racist, murderer, and war monger as Chancellor and then Führer of Germany. In contrast, consider the example of Mother Teresa (Agnes Gonxha Bojaxhiu, 1910-1997), raised in Romania, joining a group of nuns in Ireland, and then heading an order of nuns in India whose mission was to bring food, sanitation, and dignity to the impoverished dying so they might know the love of Christ before they died. Humble beginnings perhaps, but she is the only nongovernmental, nonpolitical figure to whom the government of India gave a State Funeral.

The appearance of Mary and Joseph in the temple to consecrate their Son, Jesus, to God, bespoke an *openness of heart* to the Divine Will rather than a merely *pro forma* act undertaken simply because *it was the thing to do*, a behavior perhaps devoid of understanding and certainly empty of commitment. How do I know this? How? Because Mary and Joseph had already displayed their commitment to the Divine Will: When the angel, Gabriel, told Mary that God wished her to be the mother of Jesus she completely abandoned herself to what God wanted of her ("I am the slave girl of the Lord.") and St. Joseph surely committed himself to the duties of foster-father to Jesus after an angel assured him that Mary's pregnancy came from the Holy Spirit.

All of which shows that to consecrate oneself or another to a transcendent ideal is to seek to identify the self with that ideal and thus to embody it in one's very being. It is to open one's self to the higher realities of Truth, Beauty, Goodness, and Being. Practically speaking, it is to enter the world of *commitment*. So, the formula is a simple one:

Observation, Obedience .... and *Commitment*

The French Existentialist philosopher and playwright Gabriel Marcel (1889-1973) calls our attention to the ethical and social significance of the distinction between *observation and testimony.* What emerges from Marcel's distinction is the connection between *testimony* and the *obedience of commitment.*[30] But before going any further, I'd like you to join me for a few minutes in conducting a *thought experiment.*

It's 1 AM, and I'm walking the streets in my neighborhood, unable to sleep because of an essay that I'm having trouble writing. As I step off the curb to cross the street, an automobile runs the red light, colliding with an auto that had the right of way. The errant driver is apparently unscathed, but the driver who had the green light is injured. I seem to be the only witness. I call 911, and soon a police car and ambulance arrive. I tell the police officers what I witnessed, and they proceed to gather the pertinent data, e.g., taking measurements of the skid marks from the tires of the two autos, etc.

Several days later, an official hearing of the incident takes place, and I have been subpoenaed. The police officer

---

[30] Excerpts from Gabriel Marcel, "Testimony and Existentialism," in *The Philosophy of Existentialism.* (Posted by Mélanie V. Walton, December 27, 2013). http://www.aquestionofexistence.com/Aquestionofexistence/Existentialism./Entries/2013/12/27_Gabriel_Marcel.html

who gathered the data relevant to the scene of the collision was taken to the hospital for an emergency appendectomy the day before the hearing, and a police officer, who did not participate in making the observations, had to present them at the hearing from the written accident report.

The results of *observation* can be presented accurately by anyone, even by someone who did not witness the event or had no part in directly collecting the data, provided that the data have been accurately recorded. But *testimony* can only be given by the person who directly experienced the event in question.

Consider: I alone witnessed the accident. Only I can state that I saw auto *A* go through the red light and collide with auto *B*. The most that anyone other than me can say is something like, "The skid marks show that the driver of Auto A was driving over the speed limit and abruptly applied his breaks shortly after entering the intersection, colliding with the right side of Auto B in the middle of the intersection" or "Dennehy *claims* that he saw auto *A* go through the red light and collide with auto *B*."

Testimony, it is clear, cannot be made on my behalf by another person. Only *I* can give testimony since it's a commitment that validates one's self as a *unique* center of conscious, autonomous, moral being—its obedience to the demands of testimony bespeak a commitment to serve truth and goodness. The driver who ran the red light is the son of a very wealthy, influential figure in the city. Will he use his influence to retaliate against me for fingering his son as the errant driver? Should I lie to avoid the possibility of harm? I am free to choose to lie or tell the truth. I resolve to tell the truth. My obedience to the demands of truth and goodness enables me to transcend the contractions and limitations of self to embrace the wider realms of truth and justice.

When Mary said "Yes" to God's invitation to be the mother of His son, she did what nobody could do on her behalf. Without God, Mary was powerless to attain redemption for mankind; but her testimony/commitment and obedience joined her with God's infinite power: she gave birth to the God-man, the Savior of the world. And Mary and Joseph's consecration of the child, Jesus, to God in the temple, reaffirmed (*deepened*) their obedience, testimony, and commitment.

Christ was frightened during his last hours as he prayed in Gethsemane. He begged His Father in Heaven to let Him walk away from the task before Him: "Father, if it be Thy will, let this chalice pass from Me." But He quickly affirmed His obedience with the words, "Not My will, Father, but Thine be done." The God-man affirmed His choice to suffer and die for our sins, thereby embracing all creation in His unique self.

St. Peter chose the opposite course. Instead of testifying to the truth, he chose to lie, saying, when identified as a follower of Christ, that he didn't know Him. But that lie collided with his sense of self, with the *I* who Peter knew himself—and wanted himself—to be. His repentance washed his face with tears. He renewed his obedience and would go to his execution as a proud disciple of Christ, requesting of his executioners that they crucify him upside down as he was unworthy to emulate the death of his beloved Redeemer.

All of which reveals the link between *testimony* and *commitment*: we must commit ourselves to the truth of an event or proposition as a condition of *testifying* to its truth. In other words, we must be *obedient* to the truth.

THE 5ᵀᴴ JOYFUL MYSTERY

Mary and Joseph find the Child Jesus in the Temple

One commentary on this mystery invites us to focus on the following: "I will look for Christ in all situations, even the most improbable." In the post-Resurrection Gospel, Christ instructs His disciples to go forth and teach all nations what He has taught them and adds that they need not fear that their audiences might harm them. Why? Because "I am with you all days, even till the end of the earth." Observing their twelve-year-old son explaining scripture to the temple elders baffled Mary and Joseph. Who could deny that the situation confronting them was *improbable?*

> "When his parents saw him, they were astonished, and his mother said to him, "Son, why have you done this to us? Your father and I have been looking for you with great anxiety." And he said to them, "Why were you looking for me? Did you not know that I must be in my Father's house?" But they did not understand what he said to them." (Luke 2: 48-50, NAB)

Importantly, the question arises: A twelve-year-old knows more about the Sacred Texts than do the teachers?

When Christ says that He's always with us, He means *always*. Knowing that He has our backs trumps by far not knowing it, even when we aren't sure or don't even have a hint of what He wants us to do because He'll let us know. For example, a priest once told me that he was a soldier in the United States Army and that, when World War II ended, he was hoping and praying for an early discharge back into civilian life. That never happened, and he was understandably disappointed. Eventually, he realized that if he had been discharged early, he would never have become a priest. By not getting an early discharge, it seemed *impro-bable* to him that it would be the happier outcome, but Christ *had his back* and was with him all along, leading him to the job of his life's fulfillment.

What about when the bad times don't go away? When it goes on like that it's because of one or more of a number of reasons. For example, (1) Christ is, to borrow my son-in-law, Steve's term, *refining* us; (2) We may be praying for the right outcome, but failing to cooperate with God by using the right human means to attain it; for example, consistently getting low grades in one's college courses despite praying for better grades but not studying as much as necessary; (3) Unhappiness with one's occupation. When I was in graduate school and soon to be married, I got a job that summer as an "Accounting Assistant" with a major oil company. Not only did I dislike that kind of work, but for two consecutive months, a more experienced employee had to be assigned to check my account books for mistakes, and there were many mistakes. Clearly, accounting was not my cup of tea. I submitted my resignation at the end of August and resumed my graduate studies in philosophy.

And sometimes we have a job that we're good at but doesn't make us happy. That could be God nudging us to look in a different direction for our occupation, one that He created us for.

I was a feckless adolescent. In high school, I barely studied any of my courses as my dismal monthly report cards reflected. For that academic inadvertence, I was "grounded," and the only social life my parents permitted was Friday evenings at my Boy Scout meetings. After high school—how I managed to graduate continues to baffle me—I worked at flunky clerical jobs, the first at Southern Pacific Railroad and the second at Pacific Telephone and Telegraph Company. My only interest, then, was competitive Olympic style weightlifting. I managed to win second place in the light-heavyweight class of the Pacific Coast A.A.U. contest, but when I presented my father with my medal, he couldn't believe it, responding in a tone dripping with incredulity: "Second Place in the *whole* Pacific Coast, Raymond?"

Joining the Navy two years after I graduated from high school was at the time, I now believe, my most important decision. My father didn't want me to join, but my mother encouraged it. I spent four years aboard the heavy cruiser, USS Rochester, CA 124, as a radarman. This meant that I would spend a lot of time in the "radar shack" (the Combat Information Center) chatting with the officer on duty there, especially on the mid-watch (midnight to 4 AM) when our ship was crossing the Pacific Ocean with hardly anything of naval interest showing up on the radar. From those conversations with officers, I decided that I wanted to be "sharp" and to make something of myself, starting by going to college. This desire to be "sharp" derived momentum from showing the officers and my fellow sailors that I was intelligent and responsible as I advanced in rating from Seaman Apprentice, to Seaman, to Radarman 3rd Class, to Radarman 2nd Class, but failed the test (these were fleetwide examinations) for Radarman 1st Class, which required skill with applied trigonometric functions (mathematics has always been my weakest subject).

Several months later, I declined a second opportunity to take the test, my reasoning being that my four-year enlistment was almost finished, and I was planning to attend college; I worried that because 1st Class Petty Officers have such prestige that, if I passed the test, I might decide to re-enlist and not go to college. In retrospect, I can't help but wonder whether my decision not to retake the test for 1st class was the result of Jesus watching my back.

By consecrating their son, Jesus, to God in the temple ceremony, Mary and Joseph were following Jewish tradition. As humdrum as submission to tradition may seem, it can furnish the context for self-fulfillment and even heroic action by pointing us in the right direction. And no direction could be "more right" than consecration to God, otherwise known as "putting God first." According to Catholic doctrine, there are three sacraments of initiation into the Catholic Church: Baptism, Holy Communion, and Confirmation. These build on one another, or, as the Catechism of the Catholic Church explains, "Confirmation perfects Baptismal grace; it is the sacrament which gives the Holy Spirit in order to root us more deeply in the divine filiation, incorporate us more firmly into Christ, strengthen our bond with the Church, associate us more closely with her mission, and help us bear witness to the Christian faith in words accompanied by deeds."[31]

As a student in Catholic grammar school and high school, I was taught that the sacrament of Confirmation brought us the Holy Spirit to make us defenders of the faith. I wouldn't have guessed it, but during my four years in the U.S. Navy, I began to develop an interest in Catholic doctrine and, once in a Catholic university, the many required theology courses greatly interested me, as did the required courses in philosophy, especially Thomistic philosophy. By the time I finished my graduate studies in philosophy and began teaching philosophy as a junior professor, I was already defending the Catholic Church's teaching on contraception, and a couple of years later found myself debating against abortion, physician-assisted suicide, and

---

[31] "Confirmation." Catechism of the Catholic Church, 1316. http://www.vatican.va/archive/ENG0015/__P3V.HTM

homosexuality, and on one occasion, defending *Humanae Vitae* in a public debate against the Jesuit Chairman of the Theology Department at my university. And, more recently, I engaged in a public debate at the university against a gay Anglican priest on the Catholic Church's teaching on homosexuality. Judging from the campus police in the audience that evening, the university apparently feared trouble, but other members of the audience were also fearful. For example, I learned after the debate that, for the occasion, my wife carried pepper spray in her purse.

The point is that putting God first—getting Baptized, receiving Confirmation, and regularly receiving Christ's body and blood in the Eucharist—we open ourselves to God's plan for us.

The aforementioned meditative fruit of this Mystery, "I will look for Christ in all situations, even the most improbable," relates to another commentary that cites, as its meditative fruit, "I will keep Christ in mind in all situations. Its relation to the former commentary draws its lesson from Mary and Joseph losing track of Jesus, thinking He was with relatives when He was discussing scripture with the elders in the temple. Similarly, if **we lack a prayer life with Christ, we may, out of habit, fail to think of Him or call upon Him when we need Him.**

"When I lose Jesus in my daily life, do I go frantically searching for Him like I would my lost child? Do I know

where to find Him? Do I go straight to the obvious place to look for Him?"

"I pray that in those times when I feel like I have lost Jesus Christ in my life I realize that He has not lost me. I pray that I remember where to find Him at all times—He is busy with His Father's affairs." [32]

---

[32] "Meditations on the Joyful Mysteries," *Mary's Touch.* http://marystouch.org/how-to-pray-the-rosary/joyful-mysteries

LUMINOUS MYSTERIES

THE 1ST LUMINOUS MYSTERY

The Baptism of Jesus

The First Luminous Mystery celebrates the descent of the Holy Spirit on Christ. Discussions of the Holy Spirit's influence are, so far as I can tell, almost always about His influence on Sacred Scripture, Papal pronouncements, or our resolution of religious or moral questions and problems. But how about the Holy Spirit helping us through secular questions and problems?

Consider: Louis Pasteur (1822-1895) was not only a great scientist; he "showed that food spoils because of micro-organisms and invented *pasteurization*, which was originally used to prevent wine and beer from souring. If that wasn't enough, he also came up with a rabies vaccine.[33]

Pasteur was also a devout believer in God and in the power of prayer. I remember a book (title and author escape my memory) in which the author referred to the quip that Pasteur spent more time praying in church than he spent in his laboratory. At all events, it is well documented that he was frequently seen in church, praying his Rosary. Surely, many of his prayers were petitions for help with his laboratory experiments. And equally surely, the Holy Spirit

---

[33] "Louis Pasteur (1822-1895)" *Time Magazine.* http://content.time.com/time/specials/2007/article/0,28804,1677 329_1677708_1677753,00.html

illuminated for Pasteur the path to the resolution of those problems he encountered in the laboratory.

Because our reception of the sacrament of Confirmation confers the grace of the Holy Spirit, enabling us to defend our Faith, I've often wondered about the influence of the Holy Spirit on my debates on abortion, contraception, homosexuality, and euthanasia on Universities, radio, and television, spanning over 50 years. Why do I wonder? It's because I've never thought of myself as a courageous person, yet I've never feared speaking against the above practices, nor to my memory, I have not even ever thought of what people think of me for doing so. However, I have to admit that at the start of my twice-yearly abortion debates at the University of California, Berkeley Campus, I experienced anxieties while driving to their campus, but they seemed to leave as soon as I got on the debate stage. So, I have good reason, based on my own experience, for believing the Holy Spirit has been at my side in my public life.

Christ called Satan the "father of liars." One form of his ways of lying is to persuade people to believe that what is false is true, whether about religion or morality. The remedy to this form of prevarication is twofold: Prayer to the Holy Spirit and the use of available moral human means to challenge the falsities. Here the influence of the Holy Spirit evinces itself by enlightening our intellects and strengthening our wills. Defending truth requires knowing both *why* a statement is true and *confronting* false statements. Unfortunately, some people know the truth but fear making their position public; others who know the truth do not fear announcing it but have no desire to take the trouble of doing so. Such fear and reluctance increase the media's influence on the public's thinking.

THE 2ND LUMINOUS MYSTERY
The Marriage Feast at Cana

Here we get another example of what the Incarnation means. We are taught that Jesus "became like us in all things except sin." Thus, Mary was, and is, *really* His mother and Jesus was, and is, *really* her son. In my discussion of the 3rd Joyous Mystery, I had occasion to address Mary's suasion over Her Son at the Cana wedding banquet: When the wine ran out, she asked Jesus to make more wine, but He said it was not time for Him to begin His public ministry by working a miracle; nevertheless, He made more wine. Jesus, the Christ, thus displayed filial obedience to His mother, Mary, which, under the circumstances, meant working His first public miracle.

You'll come across commentaries on the Rosary that cite as the meditative fruit of this Luminous Mystery, "Through Mary to Jesus." Amen! Think of how often we pray to Mary with our requests. Permit me to quote again the words of Mother Teresa: "You cannot learn this from books, you must experience in your life, that whatever you ask Our Lady she will do…"

Jesus will always be the Son of Mary and she will always be His Mother. So, is it not safe to say that He will forever show filial respect for her? Surely. But the statement, "Through Mary, to Jesus" means just what it says. Mary gave

Jesus to the world. We get to Him through Mary, for she said "Yes" to God when she could have said "No." But we do not *worship* Mary. That would collide with the First Commandment: "Thou shalt not have strange gods before me." But, clearly, Jesus has a special mission for her in addition to being His mother—the Mother of God—as shown by the apparitions at Lourdes, Fatima, and Guadalupe.

THE 3RD LUMINOUS MYSTERY

The Proclamation of the Kingdom of God

Christ instructed His disciples to preach that "the kingdom of heaven is at hand." He also instructed them to "cure the sick, raise the dead, cleanse lepers, drive out demons." (Matthew10:8) To the best of my knowledge, I can't work miracles and don't know anyone who can. I know that miracles nevertheless do occur, as the rigorous criteria required both by the Vatican's process of canonization and the conclusion of a cure at the shrine of Lourdes report.

Does lacking the power to work miracles exclude us from showing that the kingdom of heaven is at hand? I say that it doesn't. In my discussion of the 4th Joyous Mystery, I frame the influence that one has upon other people by one's conduct. Possessing the virtues of charity, humility, and honesty won't go unnoticed. Christ is the Incarnation of God in man. His death and Resurrection have empowered us to embody His Incarnation in our lives and work; but, along with the example of our way of living, the fulfillment of His teaching that the "kingdom of heaven is at hand" requires preaching the Gospel and showing how the word of God applies to contemporary events, questions, and problems. This requirement will have difficult moments insofar as the one preaching must explain the Church's teaching on touchy subjects like premarital sex, homosexuality, contraception, and abortion, etc. A colleague of mine, at the university where I taught, left the Catholic Church, with his wife, to become Anglicans because of their shock at the appearance of the Papal Encyclical, *Humanae* vitae, which upheld the Church's teaching against contraception. And I was at a Mass when the priest delivered a sermon against abortion and, as soon as the sermon ended, a woman in a pew upfront immediately walked out of the church in what seemed, given her facial expression and determined walk, to be anger and indignation, leaving her husband in the pew.

Such casualties are unfortunate. But a pulpit that remains silent on touchy subjects risks the danger against which Christ warned: the salt loses its flavor. Salt that is no longer flavorful is discarded. Similarly, sermons that dodge addressing subjects that impact people's lives will be discarded.

The main obstacle to preaching that "the kingdom of heaven is at hand" is secularism, whose advocates seek to erase thoughts of God and personal immortality from our minds. The successes of that venture are noteworthy. In this book's Prologue, I cited the European countries that, as of 1981, make no reference to God in their constitutions. And fewer and fewer people in the United States go to church on Sundays while the Obituary section of our newspaper shows that some of the deceased are buried without religious ceremony ("As per his/ or her/ request there will be no funeral services"); and with the exception of clerical scandals, God, along with religious topics, are subjects of shrinking interest in film and media. And what has happened to so-called "Catholic" universities? The Catholic university that I attended required the student to take a course in theology every semester. Now that same school requires only one religious course, not in theology, but in *Religious Studies,* and it doesn't have to be a study of Catholic or any Christian religion; Buddhism will do.

THE 4TH LUMINOUS MYSTERY

The Transfiguration of Christ

"While he was praying his face changed in appearance and his clothing became dazzling white. And behold, two men were conversing with him, Moses and Elijah, who appeared in glory and spoke of his exodus that he was going to accomplish in Jerusalem. . . . Then from the cloud came a voice that said, 'This is my chosen Son; listen to him.'" (Luke 9:29-31, 35, NAB)

I'm inclined say that this Mystery gives a foretaste of the Kingdom of heaven and thus connects with the previous Mystery in which Christ instructs His disciples to preach that the Kingdom of heaven is at hand.

Why? The faculty of sight is our most informative sense. The sudden radiance of Christ's garments and change of His countenance showed Peter, John, and James a brightness that they would never behold in the natural world. And what about the change in His countenance? "Countenance" refers to the *expression* on one's face. The context of the above scriptural passage clearly eliminates the possibility that Christ's mood changed to anger or disapproval. Given that His clothing became radiant, surely His facial expression must have been one of joyous beatitude. Add to these that Christ took His disciples with Him up the mountain to pray and that God, the Father, spoke to them from a cloud: "This is my chosen Son; listen to him."

What do those events on Mount Tabor offer us here in the 21ˢᵗ Century? For starters, Christ's radiance tells us that life in heaven differs indescribably from what we have experienced here in our earthly existence. In the words of St. Paul: "What eye has not seen, and ear has not heard, and what has not entered the human heart, what God has prepared for those who love him." (1 Corinthians 2:9, NAB) Calling attention to the glories of heaven reveals something else. On this point, we return to the 3ʳᵈ Luminous Mystery where Christ exhorts His disciples to preach that the kingdom of heaven is at hand. One commentary on that Mystery is that its spiritual fruit is "Christian Witness and Conversion."[34]

The question is *How do we persuade America, along with other Christian countries, to return to God?* The advances of secularism, even in its muscular form, don't extinguish hope. For example, in an email that arrived on the day I'm writing this (3-17-20) came a report that 24 counties in Latin America have thanked President Trump for his public stand against abortion. Here I must risk repeating myself *ad nauseum*: Christian *witness* will lead to *conversion*: witness from the pulpit, the classroom, the written word, and political movement, not to mention the

---

[34] "The Luminous Mysteries," The Rosary Center. https://www.rosarycenter.org/homepage-2/rosary/how-to-pray-the-rosary/luminous-without-distractions/

personal lives of those committed to Christian virtue. We can't expect to bat a 1000 in these ventures; Christ Himself did not convert people whose hardness of heart was rebarbative to His words. But that is another example of Christianity's basis in a person's freedom. Nevertheless, our batting average can be high enough to defeat secularism. However, it won't get that high in the absence of *Christian Witness*.

THE 5TH LUMINOUS MYSTERY
The Institution of the Eucharist

"…Then he took the bread, said the blessing, broke it, and gave it to them, saying, 'This is my body, which will be given for you; do this in memory of me.' And likewise the cup after they had eaten, saying, 'This cup is the new covenant in my blood, which will be shed for you.'" (Luke 22:19-20, NAB)

In the Consecration of Holy Mass, Christ, through the priest saying the Mass, changes mere bread into His body while retaining the bread's physical properties and changes mere wine into His blood while retaining the wine's physical properties. In my senior year at the university, my theology course was about the Seven Sacraments, giving the opportunity for a close look at the Eucharistic sacrifice. As I reflect on that study, four things come to mind.

First, it allows the priest and the people to offer a sacrifice to God of infinite worth, reenacting Christ's sacrifice of Himself on the cross, to the infinite being, God the Father. Second, consuming the consecrated bread and/or wine allows the people at the Mass, along with the priest celebrating it, an intimate unity with Christ that is both physical and spiritual. Third, the institution of the Eucharist responds to the call of holiness. Receiving the Eucharist requires that the recipient be in the state of grace, which means the freedom from mortal sin. Fourth, Christ's choice of bread, which is perhaps the most common of foods consumed by humans, shows that He wished the largest number of people to have access to the Eucharistic sacrifice.

SORROWFUL MYSTERIES

THE 1ST SORROWFUL MYSTERY

Christ's Agony in the Garden

The Loneliness of the Long-Distance Runner

I recall watching a television newscast of Fidel Castro's soldiers, who, after having taken over the Cuban government (1959), they lined up the defeated Baptista officials and executed them by firing squad. Before their execution, blindfolds were placed on them, but one of the doomed men refused that consideration, as if to display his contempt for Castro's Communist soldiers and to show courage in the face of death. He was an example of the truth that not all people fear death. Some people welcome, and even initiate, their death. Consider, for example "assisted suicide," the most common form being when a patient requests the physician to end his life by administering a lethal chemical to him. A less common form of assisted suicide is what is called "suicide by cop," where a man deliberately provokes a gun fight with police so they will kill him in the exchange. And San Francisco's Golden Gate Bridge offers an apparently romanticized suicide. More than 1,600 people have leaped to their deaths since the bridge opened in 1937.

Realistically, suicide is almost always motivated by physical or emotional pain if not a fear of exposure for the commission of a crime or degrading and humiliating behavior: an incurable disease, an elderly patient's belief that he or she is a financial or emotional burden to the family, a rejected suitor who believes that life is not worth living without the woman he wished to marry, or a fear of discovery that one has molested a child, etc.

The Center for Disease Control (CDC) noted that, "More than half of people who died by suicide did not have a known mental health condition."[35] At all events, some people are *determined* to end their lives. I once read in our local newspaper of a man who committed suicide by drilling into his skull with a handheld power tool, an achievement that apparently required *eight* attempts!

What about people who love life, have no desire to die, and yet who *put their lives on the line* for the sake of others? For example, a young man who enlists in the army because he believes he has an obligation to defend his country in time of war? A husband who throws himself in front of his wife to protect her from someone wielding a dagger? A young woman who rushes into a burning home to rescue a child? And what about a thirty-three-year-old man, apparently in good health, who has chosen, out of love, to suffer the excruciating pain of whipping, the public humiliation of

---

[35] "Suicide Rising Across the US," Center for Disease Control. Sourcing from the National Center for Injury Prevention and Control. (June 7, 2018)
https://www.cdc.gov/vitalsigns/suicide/index.html

coarse people spitting on Him, blaspheming His Kingship, and a horrible death by crucifixion?

I'm reminded of a short story by Alan Sillitoe, published in 1959 and adapted for a 1962 film with the same title.[36] Why that choice? Because the long-distance runner is *alone* with his thoughts. It would, of course, be plausible to suppose that, of all the thoughts that might cross his mind while running, winning the race or at least finishing it, would be primary; but the story's central figure is a juvenile delinquent who, in one particular long-distance race, is considering ways of reforming his life. That makes sense. Running all alone without distractions for a protracted length of time could plausibly confront anybody with thoughts that have been eating at him. But whatever his thoughts might be, he has nobody there with whom to discuss them. Whatever he's thinking about, he's thinking about alone.

But, as lonely as long-distance running may be, and, indeed, even as lonely as being confined to solitary confinement surely is, could anyone have ever been lonelier than Christ in Gethsemane? Of course, two or three hours doesn't match a jail sentence in solitary. But that's to speak in terms of *quantity*, length of time, not in terms of *quality*, in choosing to suffer and die for the benefit of others. When

---

[36] Alan Sillitoe, *The Loneliness of the Long-Distance Runner* (United Kingdom, W. H. Allen Ltd., 1959).

meditating on Christ alone in that garden, I often ask Him to strengthen and comfort those who are dying all alone. Loneliness can be greatest when we know that we are dying. No matter how grief-stricken the family members and loved ones gathered around one's hospital bed may be, he or she alone is dying. Even if we were all to die at once, death is not an act that can be shared. Each of us dies alone. To be sure, there are many things, besides dying, that we must experience alone. Others may empathize with the pain or fear we suffer, but whatever their pain and its cause, *that* pain is not our pain. Considering all the experiences one can have, *dying* is a unique experience for anyone who is conscious; it's a road we walk all alone through the darkest valley of all.

All Alone in Gethsemane

"Why am I doing this?" How often have you asked yourself that question? It usually confronts us when we're engaged in a task that we'd rather not be doing, either because of our frustration when the hoped-for results continue to escape us or because the very activity of seeking those results threatens our plans or wellbeing. The profundity of Christ's agony in anticipating His death is infinite. Facing His execution, Christ is scared; so scared that he begs His Father in Heaven to spare him from death. But why should He fear dying? After all, He's God, and God can't die. Right? Right, God cannot die, but that way of looking at the

Incarnation robs it of any claim to being a *Mystery*. The Mystery is that Christ "became like us in all things but sin." He had a human consciousness, human emotions, a human imagination, and human desires; but the relation between His divinity and humanity was not a transcendental relation that allowed Him to think, "Well, it's time for me to die, but only my *human* self will die, not my *divine* self. In three days, My Father will bring my *human self* back to life." The Incarnational Mystery does not mean that the Divine Christ occupied a human body for thirty-three years and then vacated it when it died, just as one moves out of an apartment after finding better accommodations. The Incarnational Mystery is a *Mystery* because it teaches us that Christ is at once *both God* and *man*. If Christ were not both Divine and human, His willingness to suffer and die for our sins could not be fulfilled. But Christ is one, single being— two natures, one Divine, the other human, both in one and the same *person, a single substance;* theologians call this the *Hypostatic* union: "a theological term used with reference to the Incarnation to express the revealed truth that in Christ one person subsists in two natures, the Divine and the human. Hypostasis (upostasis) means, literally, that which lies beneath as basis or foundation. Hence it came to be used by the Greek philosophers to denote reality as distinguished from appearances (Aristotle, "Mund.", IV, 21)."[37] A finite mind cannot grasp how this is possible, but if it were impossible, we would not be redeemed. As God, Christ is an infinite being whose offering of Himself to God, the Father, was a sacrifice of infinite value and thus an acceptable offering of atonement for our sin against an Infinite being.

Can we even begin to imagine the intensity of Christ's agony and sense of isolation—His loneliness—that night in Gethsemane? There he kneels, engulfed by the darkening night. Peter and others were there, but even if hundreds or thousands had accompanied him to the Garden, their presence could not have overcome the bottomless depth of His loneliness. For He alone—not Peter or John or anyone else—has chosen to suffer and die that we might be saved. Christ made that choice and now the consequences of that choice, the suffering, humiliation, and death, confront Him. *How?* Not as a mere thought, as an idea logically or plausibly drawn from other ideas as in the statement, "If I, Christ, choose to assume a human nature and to suffer and die for the sins of all human beings, then they will be redeemed." On the contrary, what confronted Christ in the Garden of Gethsemane that night was the inevitable, imminent consequence of the profoundest *commitment,* actual suffering, humiliation, and *death.* What faced Christ on that

---

[37] E. A. Pace, "Hypostatic Union," Catholic Answers. https://www.catholic.com/encyclopedia/hypostatic-union

night is what the Germans call *erlebnis*, a "lived experience." As a completely human being, he was terrified at the thought of giving up His life, especially, no doubt, for people who never even knew He existed, for others who were indifferent towards Him, and for still others who hated Him. He was *terrified* and *all alone* in confronting what was about to happen to Him, but His love for us—for each of us—and commitment to suffer a painful death to atone for our sins transcended his terror.

Say what? Ok. Christ has chosen to give up his life for our salvation, even for men and women who couldn't care less about him: "Father, forgive them, they know not what they do." (Luke 23:34, NAB) How great an offense against God is sin! But for most of my life I never thought about how terrible a thing sin must be to require that an infinite being choose to give up his life to free us from its grip; nor did I think of how great His love for us must be. God loves us so greatly that He's given his life for each one of us, for *me*, Raymond Leo Dennehy, sinner that I am! Mere finite being that I am! Mediocre ability that I possess! An infinite, absolutely perfect being loves me, loves me enough to suffer and die for me. Go figure!

THE 2ND SORROWFUL MYSTERY
Christ is Scourged at the Pillar

What's it feel like to be scourged, to have the skin on your back torn **and bleeding and the open wounds continuously whipped?** I can't even imagine. As I write this, I have a corn on the sole of my right foot. The pain, when my foot is positioned in a certain way on most floor surfaces is excruciating. But, in most situations, I can quickly change the position of my foot or the surface on which I'm standing and get immediate, though not always complete, relief.

But when you're being scourged, your hands are usually tied together on the part of the whipping post that's above your head, perhaps thereby limiting your range of motion to reduce the number of times getting lashed on the opened wounds; and the repetitive pain of the lashing must seem to be endless. It will end, but it seems to go on and on. Was Christ crying from the pain? Was He screaming? Was He trying to anticipate when the whip would strike and move His torso to lessen its force? A vain effort, but in such extreme cases, one has to try something. Or maybe one would have more success psychologically by *defiantly* standing up to the pain. Decades ago, a physician named Walsh wrote a book on training the will in which he claimed that defiance to pain reduces the areas of the brain that register pain.

Apparently, some people have what, from all appearances, can only be called an "heroic toughness" to pain. Consider, for example, *Wikipedia*'s account of U.S. Navy officer Admiral Stockdale's imprisonment and torture in Viet Nam.

Prisoner of war

"On 9 September 1965, while flying from USS Oriskany on a mission over North Vietnam, Stockdale ejected from his Douglas A-4 Skyhawk, which had been struck by enemy fire and completely disabled. He parachuted into a small village, where he was severely beaten and taken prisoner.

"Stockdale was held as a prisoner of war in the Hỏa Lò Prison (the infamous "Hanoi Hilton") for the next seven-and-a-half years. As the senior Naval officer, he was one of the primary organizers of prisoner resistance. Tortured routinely and denied medical attention for the severely damaged leg he suffered during capture, Stockdale created and enforced a code of conduct for all prisoners which governed torture, secret communications, and behavior. In the summer of 1969, he was locked in leg irons in a bath stall and routinely tortured and beaten. When told by his captors that he was to be paraded in public, Stockdale slit his scalp with a razor to purposely disfigure himself so that his captors could not use him as propaganda. When they covered his head with a hat, he beat himself with a stool until his face was swollen beyond recognition. When Stockdale was discovered with information that could implicate his friends' "black activities", he slit his wrists so they could not torture him into confession. During the course of his captivity, due to torture, his leg was broken twice."[38]

Impressive? Heroically so, bordering on Homeric myth! But an important difference between what Christ and Stockwell suffered was that, apparently, many of Stockwell's injuries and physical sufferings were self-inflicted whereas none of Christ's were. I make no pretense of psychiatric competence. But it seems obvious that self-inflicted injury, when such infliction is motivated by the desire for benefit to one's self and others offers a payback that injury and pain inflicted by others can't offer because then the recipient neither initiates nor desires the injury.

I suspect it's more likely that Christ chose an altruistic stance by offering the pain of his scourging up in reparation for the sins of the flesh committed by His fellow human beings. To repeat, I won't play the role of sidewalk psychiatrist by confidently offering that explanation, but altruism does seem a fitting stance for the Redeemer of the World, not to mention the possibility of altruistic motives making the pain of scourging at the pillar more tolerable.

---

[38] "James Stockdale," Wikipedia.org.
http://en.Wikipedia.org/wiki/James Stockdale

Scourging someone is punishment, but I can't help but wonder if it does not sometimes, if not often, also express the frustration of whoever ordered the scourging and also the frustration of the one doing the scourging. For example: "In 483 BC the king of Persia, Xerxes, set out to conquer the Greek mainland. Xerxes attacked Greece to avenge the failure of his father, Darius, who lost a major battle against the Greeks at a place called Marathon about a decade earlier. In order to get his army over to Greece by land he had to build a bridge over a strait of water called the Hellespont. His engineers started construction on the bridge but before it was finished, a terrible storm came and destroyed all the progress they had made. Xerxes was so upset at what happened that he had every engineer beheaded then sent soldiers down to the banks of the strait and actually had them whip the sea 300 times for its failure to obey him and comply with his plans."[39]

Was the decision to scourge Christ motivated, at least in part, by frustration? The fact that the Romans would crown Him after the scourging suggests anger and frustration to the point of making a parody of His Kingship with a crown of thorns designed to humiliate and cause pain.

---

[39] Kris Heap, "Whipping the Sea – Where Do You Place the Blame?" *Successify!* (August 8, 2013). https://successify.net/2013/08/08/whipping-the-sea-where-do-you-place-the-blame/

THE 3RD SORROWFUL MYSTERY

Christ is Crowned with Thorns

In his book *The Hidden Persuaders,* Vance Packard tells how married men were not buying convertible cars in the numbers automobile manufacturers had anticipated. Psychologists explained this by saying that married men unconsciously identified convertible cars with having a mistress and couldn't entertain the thought of owning such a vehicle without experiencing feelings of guilt. With admirable celerity, Detroit replaced its manufacture of convertibles with *Hard Top Convertibles,* which fewer married men apparently had scruples about buying. After all, the replacing cars were not really convertibles.[40]

Understandably the ability to control human behavior by psychological manipulation is prized in fields other than advertising. For example, one goal in the basic training of United States Marines is to inculcate in young male recruits the belief that it is "glorious to die in battle." Apparently, it's a goal that succeeds in men under 24 years of age, but not so much with men over that age. Psychological manipulation can also be used for more insidious purposes. In 1956, I met a Jesuit missionary priest in Taiwan who told me that when he was released from a Shanghai prison, where he spent five

---

[40] Vance Packard, *The Hidden Persuaders.* (New York, NY: Longmans, Green and Co, Inc., 1957).

years, he couldn't even remember the *Hail Mary* prayer. Anyone familiar with the Catholic faith knows how deeply ingrained in the psyche of a Catholic that prayer is.

In Christ's time, some sense of psychic control, however meager, was no doubt understood. Why was He crowned with thorns? It's a safe bet that Barabbas wasn't so regaled before Pontius Pilate capitulated to mob appeal by freeing him from a murder charge. The crown was meant as a symbol of mockery of Christ's title, "Christ the King." There wasn't much to mock in Barabbas' behavior. But Christ was not only crowned with thorns and ridiculed by unflattering shouts from onlookers; He was spat upon. All of which was preceded by scourging at the pillar.

I once heard a psychologist say that some people "don't allow themselves to *feel pain*." I presumed that she was primarily referring to *mental* pain. There are, to be sure, some people who have conditioned themselves not to feel pain in specific parts of their body, such as *gurus* in India who reportedly have mastered the technique of avoiding bodily pain after drinking a concoction of broken glass[?] along with abrasive acidic liquids! But, while it's a common saying that *mental pain* can be more painful than *physical pain*, this may presuppose two different senses of the word, *pain*. Did Christ suffer more from the scourging or from the crowning with thorns, given the obvious name-calling and spitting on Him?

The lesson for meditation given in one commentary on the Third Sorrowful Mystery is Christ's unwavering commitment to truth and ideals regardless of what people said about His beliefs and teachings. This is worth our meditation, especially in face of the current rise of secularism. People, I'm thinking of priests, teachers, and politicians, and all who have an obligation to inform the public about the truth. For example, an African Catholic priest, now in the United States, told me that "he thought that priests were afraid to speak against abortion;" when I mentioned this to an American Catholic priest, he agreed. My own experience has been that I very seldom hear criticisms of abortion from the pulpit, and the same can be said about the topics of contraception, euthanasia, homosexuality, same-sex marriage, transgenderism, premarital sex, and euthanasia, etc. And all the while, the media are increasingly bolder in their support for those practices. Christ's unwavering condemnation of immorality and His commitment to Divine truth now fade next to the glorification of the secular way of life.

To be sure, prudence is required even in defense of Christian doctrine. I talked with a young priest back East, several years ago, who told me that, having delivered a sermon against pre-marital sex at Sunday Mass, he was confronted afterwards by a married couple with their young daughter. They complained to him that their daughter was too young to hear the things he said about sexual behavior.

If memory serves me, she was about ten years of age. Surely, a speaker must take into account the age and educational background of those in the audience. But that dictate of prudence does not justify speakers, whether clergy, politicians, or university teachers, failing to explain and defend important and currently relevant topics before audiences mature enough to understand what is at issue.

The Columbine Highschool massacre in Colorado on April 20, 1999, gained infamy when two students killed 11 of their fellow students by gunfire before killing themselves. One student, a known Christian, named Cassie Rene' Bernall, was told to deny God or they would shoot her. She refused to deny Him, so they shot her dead. Unfortunately, controversy surrounds the account that she was told to deny God and affirmed His existence before getting killed. Her parents' book supports that account while one or two witnesses to the killing claim that no such conversation between Cassie and her killers happened. If true, wouldn't the parent's account be a marvelous example of "unwavering fidelity to truth and ideals" expressed by St. Paul in his Epistle: "Christ Yesterday, Christ Today, Christ Forever"?

THE 4TH SORROWFUL MYSTERY

Christ Carries His Cross

Christ Carries the Weight of Our Sins

The Romans apparently required a condemned man to carry the instrument of his own execution; to wit, a heavy wooden cross. Given the flogging they gave Christ, His weakened condition left no doubt, after He fell to the ground for the second time, that He would not survive an effort to carry His cross to the place of His execution, Mount Calvary. Being noted for their practicality, the Roman soldiers conscripted an onlooker, one Simon of Cyrene, to carry Christ's cross for the rest of the journey up the hill.

Here's a life's lesson: It's imprudent to resist demands from men wearing swords and carrying spears. Like Simon, people have burdens that they didn't choose: an alcoholic spouse, a *"rageaholic"* parent, a congenital illness, etc.; some people carry crosses they've chosen out of charity for others. The ultimate paradigmatic example is Christ who chose to become human and, not only to die for us, but to *suffer* and *die* for us.

As was not uncommon, back in the day, our parents might suggest, or even exhort us, to view persistent unpleasantries as crosses to be carried and offered up to Christ. For example, I suffered from asthma until I apparently "outgrew it" when I was sixteen years of age.

Until then, I would get, what my parents called "asthma attacks," about twice a year, to accompany bad colds. The asthma lasted about a week, during which time, I would stay home from school and get little sleep, day or night, because lying down made breathing all the more difficult. The practical solution was to sit up in bed with a couple of pillows propping up my back. The standard medications were nose drops and chest cream. In those days, medications were not so liberally dispensed. When I returned to school, I was still short of breath, but the exuberance of youth had to be given its due, and I ran about in the playground despite gasping for breath.

My asthma was an example of a "cross" that one does not choose. In contrast, getting my Ph.D. was a "cross" that I chose.

I was teaching philosophy full time at the university and raising a family while writing my dissertation. After three years, my dissertation director accepted it and presented it for public defense. Unfortunately, the two faculty members appointed to review the dissertation objected to my approach to the topic. Struggling for almost a year under the scrutiny of the principal objector, I decided to drop the topic for a different one and find another dissertation director. Almost four more years passed before I completed the second dissertation and successfully defended it.

Why did I subject myself and family to all that? First of all, I wanted to teach philosophy in the university and a

Ph.D. is the needed union card. Second, I wanted to give witness to the truth about what were then and are now contemporary topics that pertain to the life and death of democracy. What topics? Secularism, abortion, contraception, transgenderism, and euthanasia. And a university appointment is an ideal platform for addressing them. As a university professor, television and radio, universities, and print media sought me for my views—even CNN! The University of California, Berkeley, invited me on fifty-two or so consecutive semesters to debate abortion before classes of hundreds of students. So, as time passed, I understood with increasing clarity, what I had bargained for in working for a Ph.D. in philosophy. I had *chosen* to carry a cross by writing a second dissertation.

Jesus knew before His Incarnation what tortures and kind of death awaited Him, so He chose to carry his cross. He chose it from eternity. As I wrote earlier that, according to His *Hypostatic union,* we can conclude that Jesus was equally human and divine, with no diminution of either his human or divine nature. In any case, given the ancient Roman appetite for requiring condemned criminals to carry their crosses to their execution, after what was a brutal scourging, the manner of execution, along with its beatings, was probably sufficiently ritualized to be common knowledge. The crowning of Jesus with thorns was probably not a common practice, but in His case, it seems to have been intended as a mockery of His alleged kingship, a touch that would, of course, have been anticipated by Him.

Jesus also knew that the purpose of His passion and death was the redemption of every human being who ever lived, even of those who hated Him to the point of wanting to see Him dead. From this, I think it's a plausible claim that, even though Jesus' passion and death were not self-inflicted like Admiral Stockdale's, He *chose* to be born of a woman and to enter a mission on earth that required brutal beating and a horrible death for the benefit of humankind and thus for the fulfillment of His love for us.

THE 5TH SORROWFUL MYSTERY
CHRIST IS CRUCIFIED

Love for another person consists of willing that person's good for his or her own sake. Christ chose to suffer and die that we might be free from sin and enjoy eternal life with Him. Christ gave up his life for us. In precise terms, He gave up his life that we may have life in abundance. That sacrifice was great because Christ is both God and man.

Consider atonement: Because Christ was human, he could die; because He was God, the offering of His life was a sacrifice of *infinite* value and thus a worthy atonement for sin against an *infinite* being, God, the Father. The infinite nature of a sacrifice needed to atone for sin tells us that the effrontery of disobeying divine commandments—committing sin—is an outrage so colossal as to beggar all possible human understanding.

Consider love: Despite the colossal outrage of sinning against God, His love for us is boundless in its infinity. So, Christ, God, the Son, chooses to suffer and die for us, thereby unlocking the gates of eternal life for you and me. The death He chose for Himself was painful and bloody. Again, Christ didn't simply die for us; He *suffered* and died for us.

Perhaps Christ's words while on the cross offer us the key to understanding why He chose a violent bloody death: "My God, My God, why have you forsaken me?" and "Forgive them Father, for they know not what they do. Even though

He has chosen to suffer and die for our sins, the sense of abandonment that plausibly accompanies Christ's violent but slow death produces a sense of *aloneness* that can be understood only in terms of the *hypostatic union*.

Christ is equally *fully* God and *fully* man, but also one, single self. As I wrote in my chapter on Christ's agony in Gethsemane Garden, if Christ were two persons, a human person and a Divine Person, His "suffering" would have been a sham.

GLORIOUS MYSTERIES

THE 1ST GLORIOUS MYSTERY

The Resurrection of Christ

"Is that all there is, is that all there is? If that's all there is my friends, then let's keep dancing. Let's break out the booze and have a ball. If that's all there is."

We're born, we live, we die. We don't ask to be born and, usually, we don't ask to die; it's the in-between, called *living,* when we start writing our "wish list." Most people don't want to die, but the number of those who do is increasing. It's called "physician-assisted suicide," a term that is often cloaked by euphemisms like "compassionate care." I've debated supporters of legalized suicide on television and college campuses. As our society becomes more secular, living loses its luster. We see that life is "a vale of tears" and otherwise humdrum. We start relying on alcohol and drugs to get us through the days and nights. The film actor, George Sanders, one of Zsa Zsa Gabor's many ex-husbands, was found dead in his hotel room in Spain, leaving a suicide note containing the sentence, "You see, life has become so very boring." That sentence is reminiscent of the song, quoted at this chapter's beginning: *"Is that all there is, is that all there is? If that's all there is my friends, then let's keep dancing. Let's break out the booze and have a ball. If that's all there is."*

Sanders' answer was "Yes, that's all there is," but perhaps the party and dance and booze couldn't allay the boredom anymore.

My own experience with death has been, on the one hand, detached and on the other hand, a bit too close for comfort. The detached experiences came from my Irish heritage. My father was from Ireland and so were both my mother's parents. Growing up going to funerals and wakes, looking down at dead human beings, was a common experience, as was listening to adults tell tales of having seen ghosts and reporting visitations from departed relatives. I recall my mother expressing skepticism about this Irish lore and my father replying, "Wasn't I after hearing the wail of the Banshee when my father died?"

The "too close for comfort" experiences occurred twice. The first happened when I was in the U.S. Navy, a Radarman, Petty Officer 2nd Class, stationed aboard a heavy cruiser sailing in the South China Sea. Our ship was running from a typhoon and we finally entered the harbor in Keelung, Taiwan, to wait for the storm to pass. When our radar picked up the typhoon heading into our harbor, we knew we had to get out of there, and fast.

On that early morning, I was the petty officer in charge of the midnight to 4 AM radar watch. As we headed out of the harbor our surface search radar blew a fuse. That radar was crucial to getting the ship safely out of the harbor since the darkness of night, combined with the storm's high winds and rain, reduced visibility to a dangerous level. Because the console with the blown fuse was in the ship's superstructure, I had to go up a few decks to replace the fuse. (The Combat Information Center—our radar room—was four decks below the main deck.) Having replaced the fuse and calling down to the radar room to make sure the surface search radar was working again, I found that I couldn't exit the compartment. Some dutiful sailor from the deck force had apparently "dogged" the hatch while I was changing the fuse, and I would need the equivalent of a pipe wrench to open it. I managed to find a hatch that wasn't dogged, only it took me outside into the powerful wind, heavy rain, and darkness. I won't hide the fact that I was scared as I descended on the wet, slippery metal ladder to the main deck. There, I had to walk gingerly on the rain-soaked, windswept teakwood deck; I was praying with every cautious step, asking God to protect me from sliding overboard. Who survives going overboard in a typhoon, especially in the darkness of night? Finally, I came to a dogged hatch that I could open without using a wrench. And in a few minutes, I was back with my shipmates among the radar screens—damp but alive. Looking back on that experience, I'm sure my memory images exaggerate the size of the ground swells of the harbor's dark waters, for they look 40 feet high, even now, over half a century later.

My second "too close for comfort" experience with death was *really* too close: I came within five minutes of choking to death. I awakened one Friday morning, a few years ago, with a strange feeling and strange sounding sore throat. After examining my throat, the physician diagnosed it as a garden variety throat infection and was going to send me home with a supply of TYLENOL. Fortunately for me, my wife had the day off work and accompanied me to the physician's office. She expressed concern to the physician by explaining that I never got sore throats, and, besides, my voice never sounded so "weird." So, the physician made an immediate appointment for me to visit the Ear, Nose, & Throat Department. That physician's examination led to a different diagnosis: "Epiglottitis." She instructed us to get me to the Emergency Room immediately and that I should be prepared to spend several days in Intensive Care.

An Ear, Nose, and Throat surgeon was waiting for me in the ER, and by then I was struggling for breath. My wife recalls the hospital staff rushing me down the hallway in a gurney to Surgery, shouting "Emergency," "Move out of the way!" After a failed attempt to intubate me so I could breathe, the surgeon succeeded in the tracheotomy. It was a couple days later that I learned I was then about five minutes away from choking to death.

What struck me about this second encounter with death was that, although I'm a Christian, I can't recall myself, anytime during the ordeal, praying or thinking about God; all that was on my mind was running away. "Running away" from what? My choking? Good luck with that.

I've just described two examples where death was staring me in the face. But more often than not, it creeps up on us from, behind: The philosopher, George Santayana, describes it this way: the animal is about to close its jaws on its prey when an avalanche buries it with its jaws still wide open. "You know neither the day nor the hour."[41]

But, no matter how it happens, each of us must die. When we're young, we don't think much about the inevitability of our death; we feel "bulletproof." That illusion evaporates as the years unfold. Some of us accept the inevitability of our death with grace; some of us do not. In Evelyn Waugh's novel *Brideshead Revisited,* one of the characters attributes their dying uncle's tenacious refusal to die, not to a will to live but to *a fear of dying.*

It's one thing if death means eternal life and quite another if it means eternal oblivion. Imagine a young couple, recently graduated from the university and more recently married. They enjoy each other's company immensely, move in "fun" social circles, and have leased a condominium on San Francisco's Embarcadero that offers a spectacular view of the bay. What's more they have entered "exciting" professions: he's training to be a stockbroker and she's starting her own catering service. And a little more frosting on the cake is always welcome: they've managed to afford a

---

[41] George Santayana, *Skepticism and Animal Faith.* (Mineola, NY: Dover Books, 1923).

snappy looking sports car (albeit "pre-owned"). Life is good, in fact, "great," until…

Until *what?* Until his wife is permanently paralyzed from the neck down when an out-of-control "eighteen-wheeler" truck veered into their sports car while they were driving home after a day at the beach. He escaped with slight injuries. But their fate was sealed: no more making love, no children, no socializing or going on the town, or having her own business…And he would have to take care of her. When he came home from the office, he would sit with her and they would talk—when she felt up to it.

His view of life was mainly secular. It wasn't that he didn't believe in God or immortality; he "supposed" that God and personal immortality were "probably" true; it was just that he didn't think about them very much.

Despite his borderline agnosticism, it is possible that he might continue to love his wife and maintain his commitment to stay and take care of her. But it is also possible—and perhaps arguably more plausible—that in time he would leave her, divorce her, to regain the life that the highway accident stole from him, a life with a loving partner with whom he might have children and would join him in moving in the social circles he loved.

The latter possibility comes with a primal rationale: What would he gain by remaining with his now paralyzed wife? His hazy view of God and the afterlife does little to stiffen any resolve he may have to stay by her side. In fact, practically speaking, his daily life may hardly differ from that of a professed atheist; he's what the philosopher, Jacques Maritain, called a "practical atheist." If his daily life and choices are pretty much the same as one who believes this life on earth is the only life he can count on, and that death will bring him no rewards or consolations for fidelity to his convalescent wife, wouldn't it then make sense for him to echo the song popularized by singer Peggy Lee?

(The form of this song is reminiscent of the technique used in expressionist German opera where both singing and talking are used; in the following song, the descriptive passages are spoken and the refrain – "Is that all there is..." – is sung.)

I remember when I was a very little girl, our house
caught on fire.
I'll never forget the look on my father's face as he gathered
me up
In his arms and raced through the burning building out to
the pavement.
I stood there shivering in my pajamas and watched the
whole world go up in flames.
And when it was all over I said to myself,
"Is that all there is to a fire?"

Is that all there is?
Is that all there is?

If that's all there is my friends
Then let's keep dancing
Let's break out the booze and have a ball
If that's all there is

And when I was 12 years old, my daddy took me to a circus.
"The Greatest Show On Earth."
There were clowns and elephants and dancing bears.
And a beautiful lady in pink tights flew high above our
heads.
And as I sat there watching, I had the feeling that
something was missing.
I don't know what, but when it was over,
I said to myself,
"Is that all there is to a circus?"

Is that all there is?
Is that all there is?
If that's all there is my friends
Then let's keep dancing
Let's break out the booze and have a ball
If that's all there is.

And then I fell in love, with the most wonderful boy in the
world.
We would take long walks by the river
Or just sit for hours gazing into each other's eyes.

We were so very much in love.
Then one day, he went away and I thought I'd die.
But I didn't.
And when I didn't I said to myself,
"Is that all there is to love?"

Is that all there is?
Is that all there is?
If that's all there is my friends, then let's keep dancing
Let's break out the booze and have a ball
If that's all there is

I know what you must be saying to yourselves.
"If that's the way she feels about it why doesn't she just end
it all?"
Oh, no, not me.
I'm in no hurry for that final disappointment.
'Cause I know just as well as I'm standing here talking to
you,
That when that final moment comes and I'm breathing my
last breath
I'll be saying to myself-

Is that all there is?
Is that all there is?
If that's all there is my friends
Then let's keep dancing

Let's break out the booze and have a ball
If that's all there is.

(This song was written and produced by Jerry Leiber and
Mike Stoller in the 1960s.)

His response to the drastic change in his marital situation might well have been different had he seriously believed and lived in the reality of an afterlife. Then he would have been able to see that enduring the hardships and pains of his life on earth would not go unrewarded, given that Christ offers everyone eternal happiness after death. Until His death and resurrection, the world "lay in sin and error pining"; Satan had a firm grip on things. Christ's Resurrection did not end the consequences of Original Sin: sickness, pain, death, natural disasters, and immoral behavior. What His Resurrection accomplished was to terminate Satan's control over nature, giving us the power to make a salvific difference in the world and, after death, to look forward to a life of eternal happiness: "What eye has not seen, and ear has not heard, and what has not entered the human heart, what God has prepared for those who love him." (1 Corinthians 2:9, NAB) Before His ascension into Heaven, Christ instructed His Apostles to "go forth and teach all nations" in His name and not to fear what others might do to them, for He would "be with them all days, even to the ends of the earth." This was a proclamation that, thanks to His death and Resurrection, we will now have a power over nature previously unattainable, including the conquest of death.

But what should be seen as an alarming reality is that the influence of secularism continues to advance, while the influence of religion grows weaker and concepts that are crucial to the rational basis of human dignity, happiness, progress, and democratic freedom, wither on the vine. What are these "crucial" concepts? Several examples: the existence of an all-powerful, all-knowing, all-good and all-loving God; that all human beings are created in His image and likeness; that after death, each of us has a destiny with Him and the opportunity to live in eternal happiness.

Absent those concepts, what's left is the concept of a life that inevitably ends in a death that means *eternal oblivion*. Therein lies the greatest insult and demoralization of all: How did it happen that rational beings should exist at all, men and women who aspire to ever better things, who seek truth, justice, beauty, and love only to die, just as dumb animals die? One Harvard evolutionist claimed that thoughts of death don't occur to animals and that it is only when the brain sufficiently enlarges, as ours did, that such thoughts present themselves. And despite its message of complete and final termination, *death* is apparently just another item in our mind's panoply of concepts. A common claim of materialists, e.g., Marxists, and other Humanists, is the fact that our death means eternal oblivion and that this doesn't lessen the benefits that each generation of human beings can achieve for the generation that follows. So, we are to believe that the existing generation of humans experience a compensatory fulfilment from an altruistic sense of benefitting future human beings. To counterbalance the knowledge of forthcoming inevitable, eternal oblivion, they must gin up their altruism to match that of Sidney Carton, Charles Dickens' character in his novel, *A Tale of Two Cities,* so they can say with some conviction, "It's a far, far better thing that I do, than I have ever done; it's a far, far better rest that I go to than I have ever known." Carton had hoodwinked the French guards into taking him to the guillotine rather than Charles Darnay.

But neither celebrations of altruism nor "Live until you die" resolutions can palliate, let alone sweeten, the colossal insult and demoralization of offering rational beings— beings who are each unique centers of self-conscious, autonomous life—an ultimate future of eternal oblivion. In his book *St. Thomas and the Problem of the Soul in the Thirteenth Century* published by the Pontifical Institute of Medieval Studies in Toronto in 1934, Anton Pegis writes that the early Christians professed ignorance about our state between death and the General Resurrection beyond supposing that it was a time of sleep.[42] This beats the

---

[42] If the saints have anything to teach us as concerns their intercession, then we can assume that our own time in heaven will

breeches off *eternal oblivion*. To be a *self*, one who can say with conviction *I am I* makes thoughts of immortality hard to shake off.

It's worth noting that the eternal life that Christ offers us is not *immortality* but the *resurrection of the body*. What's the difference? Simply (but not unimportantly) the goodness of the body and the rest of the material world as opposed to the Gnostic belief that the material world, including our bodies, is the cause of all chaos and evil. The book of *Genesis* tells us that, having created the material world, God saw that it was "good." It's in the *New Testament* that Christ preaches the *resurrection of the body*, not the immortality of our spiritual souls. This differs profoundly from Socrates' Orphic (Gnostic) beliefs expressed in Plato's *Phaedo*, where he defines "philosophy" as the "art of dying" and takes death to be the "*liberation of the soul from the body*." The positive connotation of the phrases, "art of dying" and "liberation of the soul" bespeaks the undesirability of living in a body and being surrounded by a material world.

The following examples show how the Gnostic influence is gaining ground in today's culture.

1. Gender feminists claim that, although sexual differences between men and women are real, gender

---

not be one of sleep but one of acute alertness the presence of God and our capacity to assist those still on earth.

is a *social construct,* like the rules of grammar. For example, "table" in Spanish, *la mesa,* is feminine, but in German, its masculine, *der Tisch;* hence, while the *transgender movement* cannot plausibly deny the reality of sexual difference between men and women, since that is established from the moment of conception when sperm and ovum interact, each with the other, to produce an *XX* or XY genotype, they feel free to deny the ontological/biological and *pre-social* reality of maleness and femaleness.

2. The same-sex marriage lobby.
3. Abortion clinics selling fetal body parts for experimentation.

The Gnostic influence in these movements manifests itself in their implied assumption that the human body is a mere encasement or prison, impeding our effort to realize our true selves: asexual pure spirits or pure intellects living in bodies that have little or nothing to do with *what* and *who* we are.

In his Wednesday lectures at the Vatican on the theology of the body, the late Pope St. John Paul II argued that the body is just as much the person as is the soul. I think I can relate this to an experience I had as a teenager. On the city bus I rode every weekday to school, a very attractive woman in her early twenties, I would guess, would also ride, as did a male student attending the University of San Francisco, who would transfer to the bus that went to the university. On one particular trip, he got up and was standing waiting for the bus to come to his stop. He was standing by the seat where the young woman was sitting while holding the handle that was on top of the seat in front of her. I could see her looking at his hand and smiling. She clearly enjoyed what she saw.

What has this to do with St. John Paul II's theology of the body? The pleasure the young woman got from looking at the young man's hand did not mean that she wanted to have large, masculine hands like his, but it did mean that she was drawn to them. Similarly, the pleasure a man gets from looking at a woman's hands does not mean that he wishes to have small, delicate hands like hers, but he is drawn to them. The *feminine person* that she is involves a body as well as a soul, and the *masculine person* that he is involves a body as well as a soul; more precisely, the body and the soul comprise not two substances, but one. He and she are not souls or intellects that use bodies, as Plato taught; each is an integral composite of body and soul. As Thomas Aquinas argued, to separate body and soul causes bodily decay and spiritual/intellectual immobility.

What about the gender feminists and the same-sex lobby, not to mention the transgender supporters? The clergy, academics, intellectuals, and politicians must be ready to give witness. But not to worry. Christ is risen!

THE 2ND GLORIOUS MYSTERY
Christ Ascends into Heaven

"When you walk through a storm, hold your head up
high and don't be afraid of the dark."

This imperative comes from the first line of a song in the
Broadway musical *Carousel* (later, a film) and is a
secularized version of *Psalm 23:4;* 'Even though I walk
through the dark valley of death, because you are with me, I
fear no harm. Your rod and your staff give me courage." The
big difference, of course, is that the *Psalm* version gives a
reason for not fearing "the *Dark*"—God's providential love
for us. Christ reiterates that Divine assurance in His post
Resurrection commission of His Apostles: "All power in
heaven and on earth has been given to me. Go, therefore, and
make disciples of all nations, baptizing them in the name of
the Father, and of the Son, and of the holy Spirit, teaching
them to observe all that I have commanded you. And behold,
I am with you always, until the end of the age." (Matthew
28:19-20, NAB).

Carrying out Christ's command of missionary
dedication would be dangerous, but He assured His apostles
that, whatever the dangers, He would be with them—always.
By His death and Resurrection, Christ conquered the world,
ending Satan's control over nature, and making all things
new. Since His conquest didn't erase the *effects* of Original

Sin but promised that they would not triumph. So how was nature made new?

Thanks to Christ's triumph over fallen nature, we have a new power over that nature: democratic government, natural rights, and scientific advance are three examples of how Christianity conferred on us a clearer vision of man, nature, and the universe. To wit, with the understanding that because God is the only absolute authority in the universe, western civilization arrived at the truth that no human being has absolute authority over any rational adult human; and generational meditation on Christ's exhortation to love our neighbor as ourselves (even if he is our enemy) eventually led to the doctrine of natural rights. By His death and Resurrection, Christ conquered the world, won it back from Satan, and made all things new. By ending Satan's grip on the world, we now have the power to make a difference on this earth, which, in addition to bringing Christ's saving power to humankind, enables us to transform it and its institutions into a better place. While spreading Christ's words to people in other parts of the world—the primary purpose of which is to show the way to salvation—scientific method and democracy were discovered. Consider Fr. Stanley Jaki, SJ's explanation that Christ's incarnation made modern science possible because it taught us that there's an order to creation that can be studied and understood.

Thereby hangs a tale—a tale of two misconceptions, one an anemic construal of humility that leads to what the medieval theologians called "tempting God," the other a prideful illusion that we can forcefully take over from God.

Tempting God

Consider the example of a man crossing the Atlantic on an ocean liner. It seems that, having leaned too far over the guard rail to snap a better picture of the ocean sunset, he fell overboard. While treading water to keep afloat, he prayed, "God, I do not fear drowning, for I place my trust in you." Several of the ship's crew threw him lifesavers with ropes attached to pull him back to the ship. He shouted to them, "Lifesavers aren't necessary; I put my trust in God"; next, a lifeboat came to him, which he also rejected, saying, "I don't need a lifeboat; I put my trust in God"; then a helicopter hovered over him, dropping a rope ladder for him to climb; again, he rejected help, saying he didn't need a helicopter because he put his trust in God; finally, he drowned. Once in heaven, the man said to St. Peter, "I don't understand why I drowned, I put my trust in God." St. Peter replied: "Yes, we know, and God sent you three lifesavers, a lifeboat, and a helicopter."

The moral of the story is that while prayer is always necessary, we must also use available and reasonable *human means*. It is important to bear in mind that Christ's redemption of the world is Incarnational—He used *human means*. He chose to become *human*: the Holy Spirit came upon Mary and she conceived, meaning that Christ began His human life as a zygote, went through the embryonic stage, then the fetal, infant, and adolescent stages, finally growing into a human adult. Along the way, "He grew in wisdom and knowledge," and learned the art of working with wood from His carpenter father, Joseph. God does work miracles, but the Catholic Church is very slow to label an event "miraculous." Why? Because any event that qualifies as a "miracle" requires a suspension of the laws of nature. That is why at the sacred shrine in Lourdes where ailing people go, many of whom have illnesses that the medical profession judges to be hopeless, a team of physicians examines the patient before he or she enters the grotto's waters, and if a cure is claimed, they examine the patient again for verification. As a matter of policy, "if the case appears to be serious, the physician convenes a 'Bureau', i.e. a meeting for 'discussion of a clinical case'; all doctors and healthcare workers present in Lourdes at that time can attend the meeting, *regardless of their religious belief* (italics mine).[43] I'm told that miraculous cures are rare, but even then, the Church approves of labeling as *miraculous* only a fraction of the cures cited by the physicians. I remember giving a public lecture on physician-assisted suicide when, during the question-and-answer period, a

---

[43] "The Medical Bureau of the Sanctuary." Lourdes Sanctuaire. https://www.lourdes-france.org/en/medical-bureau-sanctuary/

member of the audience said that "the first thing a person with a life-threatening illness should do is go to Lourdes." I replied that the first thing that patient should do is *both* pray and seek medical help. The Russians have an appropriate saying: "Pray, but keep rowing the boat." Failing to take appropriate action when it is available comes under the heading of "tempting God." Other examples would be praying for better grades in school, but failing to follow a reasonable study regime, or excessive drinking before driving home, but praying that God will protect one from having an accident or getting stopped by the police, etc.

A Hostile Takeover

We've all grown up with warnings that too much of anything is harmful. Greek mythology tells us that Icarus fell to his death after flying too close to the Sun. He flew that high because he *could*, not because he *should*. What about too much freedom? Is that like flying too close to the Sun? There is a parallel: Too much freedom in a democracy can lead to anarchy and even totalitarianism. Above, I said that Christianity discovered democracy. Granted, towards the end of the 5th Century B.C., democracy was established in Athens, but around 460 B.C., under the rule of Pericles, it started morphing into an aristocracy, leading to the evaporation of democratic ideals, as belief in the superiority of one-man rule gained support.

In contrast, as stated above, the democracy that we in Western culture know has its source in the Christian doctrine that God is the only absolute authority, which means that no human being has the right to dominate absolutely the life of any other adult human being. Sailing to America from Great Britain in search of *religious* freedom in the 17ᵗʰ century, the religious dissenters formed a government that flowered into democracy. Note that the result of an atheistic culture—e.g. the former Soviet Union, today's Cuba and China—is totalitarianism. This is predictable. Diminution of belief in a Supreme Being inevitably leads to a weakening in the rationale for human rights, leading government to suppose that it has license to enter ever more deeply into the lives of its people. (See the collection of essays in *Does Human Rights Need God?*)[44] Christianity also provided the rationale for the universal doctrine of human rights. As I wrote in the previous essay, meditation on Christ's exhortation to love our neighbor— even our enemy—as we love ourselves led to the conclusion that we have a duty to respect the intrinsic dignity of all human beings.

What about technology? As *per* God's command, Noah built an ark in anticipation of the coming flood. (Genesis

---

[44] *Does Human Rights Need God?* Elizabeth Bucar & Barbra Barnett, eds. (Grand Rapids, MI: Eerdmans, 2005).

5:32-10:1) I have noted in prior chapters that Christ's death and resurrection, although atoning for Original Sin, did not erase its consequences: death, illness, immoral behavior, etc.; but it did vastly enlarge our power over nature, which is to say, our ability to discover, albeit imperfectly, the *natures* of things and to control them for our benefit. Consider the improvement of human life resulting from the advent of modern scientific method, empirical medicine, technology, and the emergence of democratic government.

The rise of technology provides a good example of how *too much freedom* leads to oppression. The "freedom of scientific experimentation" is a case in point. The infamous Tuskegee Syphilis Study extended from 1932 to 1972. Three hundred and ninety-nine African-American males were denied treatment for syphilis (e.g., some were not informed that they had tested positive for syphilis). The aim of the study was to examine, by autopsy, the effect of untreated syphilis on the human body.[45]

A utilitarian ethic (*the greatest good for the greatest number of people*) was at work here in addition to the so-called "scientific imperative": *If an experiment that promises important results can be done, then it ought to be done.* Those engaged in the study no doubt justified it by the belief

---

[45] See T. J. Benedek, "The 'Tuskegee Study' of Syphillis: Analysis of Moral versus Methodological Aspects," *Journal of Chronic Diseases*, 31, (1978): 35-50.

that it would lead to better tests for syphilis and its more effective treatment, but by implication, they also harbored a willingness to cause innocent human beings to suffer and die in the name of scientific and medical progress. No matter how altruistic or humane the study's goal, that could not erase the fact that it required the direct killing of innocent human beings, an evil fatal to democratic society.

Christianity does not hesitate to remind us that our bodies are "temples of the Holy Spirit." Unfortunately, as our culture becomes increasingly materialistic, thereby blurring the difference between material nature and human nature, the conception of man as a subject for science beckons. The current case in point is the biological revolution. Its magnitude signals a decisive breakthrough in our mastery over many of the limitations of our nature and its message is that we can create more perfect human beings. While other revolutions, such as the Industrial Revolution, were confined in their influence to our environment, advances in the biological sciences bring with them the promise of manipulating human nature even to the point of manufacturing designer humans. In the 1960s, when society gave its approval to artificial contraception and thus separated sex from conception, scientists quickly took the next step by separating conception from sex. What is the significance of that?

Its significance is that the production of human life by *in vitro* fertilization is close to becoming a commonplace as is the storage of frozen human embryos. Although some of the other projects that are frequently discussed (such as recombining DNA, along with other forms of genetic engineering and cloning) still remain far from application to human beings, their very prospect confronts us with the question highlighted in the title of Jonathan Glover's book, *What Sort of People Should There Be?* (1984) The cloning of the sheep "Dolly" conferred increasing plausibility on the possibility of someday cloning humans. However fantastic, projects like the creation of computers with human brains (cyborgs) and computers with biological parts capable of replacing themselves have proven to be "thought experiments" sufficiently fascinating to technocrats and their supporters to challenge traditional conceptions of human nature.

The urgent warnings raised by C.S. Lewis in *The Abolition of Man*, Bertrand Russell in "The Science to Save Us from Science," and Paul Ramsey in *Fabricated Man* coalesce into a clarion call: just as in Greek mythology, the sweet voices of the Sirens led sailors to their doom, so the belief in the salvific benefits of laboratory reproduction comes with an ominous price tag: only the *finest* and *most useful* will be judged worthy of the petri dish. This consideration returns our attention to the question asked by the title of Jonathan Glover's book, *What Sort of People Should There Be?* How do we determine what type of people we wish to create in our laboratories? What properties must they display to qualify as the "finest" and "most useful"?

I'd like you to take a moment to conduct another thought experiment. Since the birth of Dolly, the sheep, in 1996, there has been much talk and debate about cloning, not only in scientific and other learned circles, but also by ordinary people over the kitchen table. The laboratory cloning of Dolly was a remarkable achievement, but the process has been going on in nature for thousands of years, as is shown by the birth of twins. Twins are clones. Now here's the thought experiment.

Both the natural and laboratory means of cloning show that it is possible to produce two or more beings that are genetically the same; in other words, it is possible to produce two physically identical beings. But what it is logically impossible to do and thus will never be done is to produce two human beings for whom the personal pronoun, "I," has the same referent. Every human being is unique. Check this out by asking yourself what you mean when you use the word "I" in reference to yourself. Can you even begin to answer that question? You can enumerate your likes and dislikes, beliefs, goals, memories, etc., but inevitably you must refer them to yourself. But who or what is "yourself"? Intuitively, you know that you're unique, that there has never been and never will be another *I* that has a referent that is the same referent as your *I*.

Imagine a pair of identical twins having the same goals, likes, dislikes, and the same first and middle names, as well as the same last name. And to top things off, they insist to each other, "I am you." But no matter how dedicated each may be to *proving that* their respective *I*-s have one and same referent, they would need a direct experience of each other's referent *I, i.e., one's sense of self.* Of all the people who have existed on this earth, and the billions who now exist here, and the billions more who have yet to be here, no two of them have ever had, do not now have, or will have the same referent, *I.* One might suppose that, at one point, the molds for producing unique referent *I*-s would be exhausted and duplicate referent *I*-s, selves, would start appearing. But, as noted above, it is logically impossible to have two referent *I*-s that are identical. On the other hand, unique selves are *infinitely* possible.

The problem with the laboratory production of the "finest" and "most useful" human beings is that our models are inevitably *types* and because we are social beings, the *types* we admire are almost always socially conditioned. For example, a while back a married couple placed an advertisement in Stanford University's campus newspaper offering a large sum of money for the ovum of an athletic Caucasian female under thirty years of age. I mention this because the lapsing of laboratory reproduction of humans into stereotypical models of the "finest" and "most useful," and even the most profitable, is all but inevitable.

We breed animals according to *type*—Labrador Retrievers, for example, are prized for their ready compliance with the wishes of their human owners—as we have no reason for supposing that they are *selves*, acting autonomously from unique centers of conscious being. But the generation of *human* life tells an importantly different story. As with the production of brute animals, the production of humans involves uniting the contributed male and female chromosomes into a unique genetic combination. The possible number of these combinations is inexhaustible. We cannot therefore predict with any kind of certainty, aside from the confidence that they will be members of the human species, what our offspring will be like. Their intelligence, temperament, talents, and moral integrity, etc., remain a mystery until they are born, and more precisely until they attain maturity. This consideration is important with regard to the generation of human offspring. Because the source of human dignity and primary importance to society is his or her personhood, ontological uniqueness as a self, the attempt to valorize a human being according to a *type* necessarily excludes, to a considerable extent, the possible number of genetic combinations and thus limits the range of persons that can be conceived. And that, in turn, must progressively diminish the possibility of the unique contributions of a Socrates, St. Theresa of Avila, Beethoven, Einstein, or Mother Teresa. The quest for the "finest" and "most useful" leads to the junkpile of mediocrity.[46]

Before ascending into heaven, Christ told the apostles: "But I tell you the truth, it is better for you that I go. For if I do not go, the Advocate will not come to you. But if I go, I will send him to you. (John 16:7, NAB) That *Advocate* would be the Holy Spirit, who enlightens our intellects and strengthens our wills. Without the gifts of the Holy Spirit, we appear to be inevitably self-destructive: the more spectacular our achievements, the less do we feel the need for God. It's the Tower of Babel all over again. *Vanitas vanitatum et omnia vanitas.* The story is told of a man at the horse races who is desperate to bet on a winning horse to pay off a large debt. He puts all his money on the horse he decides has the best chance of winning. When the race starts, he begins to pray constantly to God for the horse to win. His horse pulls farther and farther in front of the other horses, and when it is clear that his horse is going to cross the finish line well ahead of the others, he looks up at the sky and says, "That's ok, God, I'll take over from here."

It's when we forget—or, more likely, choose not to bear in mind—our constant need for God's guidance that we engage in projects like the Tuskegee Syphilis Study or seek to

---

[46] See Raymond Dennehy, "The Biological Revolution and the Myth of Prometheus" the *Pope John Paul Lectures Series in Bioethics*, Vol. II, "Bioethical Issues," 1986, 7-34.

produce hybrids, part human and part pig, or conquer death through science, that we lose appreciation for who put us here, who watches over us, and who cleaned up that colossal mess called "Original Sin" by choosing to suffer and die for us. That's when we start to rebuild the Tower of Babel, again and again and again! Rather than thanking and praising God for our achievements, we decide to replace Him. I believe it's an attempt, doomed to failure, to pull off what in financial circles is called a "hostile takeover." "That's okay, God, we'll take over from here."

THE 3RD GLORIOUS MYSTERY

The Descent of the Holy Spirit on the Apostles

The Battle of Lepanto: On October 7, 1571, the fleet of the Holy League, led by the Spanish Empire and the Venetian Republic, decisively defeated the fleet of the Ottoman Empire. This was a major setback for the Muslim forces and, for all practical purposes, stopped their advances against the Christian West. Although outnumbered in sea craft and sailors, the Christian sailors prayed intensely to Mary, the Mother of God, on the eve of battle.

In 1917, in Fatima, Portugal, three shepherd children, Lucia Santos, and her cousins, Jacinta and Francisco Marto, claimed to have had visions of a "luminous lady" whom they believed to be the Virgin Mary. She promised them that, if people prayed the Rosary regularly, Communism would be defeated. Many people, across the globe, began the daily recitation of the Rosary and, after 74 years, the Communist government came to an end in Soviet Russia and its territory.

The above events are, to be sure, astounding and edifying but foretold. When God banished Adam and Eve from the Garden of Eden, He promised that the head of the serpent would be crushed by the heel of the woman. She's the *Theotokos*, the Mother of God. God, from the beginning, proclaimed that Mary would exert a decisive influence in Satan's defeat, as is clear from Sacred Scripture and Sacred Tradition.

Eve disobeyed God, and persuaded her husband, Adam, to join in the mutiny by eating the apple from the forbidden tree. In contrast, Mary's joy was to obey God: "I am the *slave girl* of the Lord."

What, you ask, has all this to do with the Third Glorious Mystery? It has a lot to do with it. Mary said "Yes" to God when He asked her to be His Mother. She *chose* through her free will to become the *Mother of God.* God doesn't play games. By enlisting her as His mother—His real mother, not a cardboard likeness—she had a mother's dignity and thus, I'm inclined to believe, a mother's authority in the celestial household.

Thus, I return to the Third Glorious Mystery (though in spirit I haven't left it). Mary is the Spouse of the Holy Spirit and the Mother of God. In the Third Glorious Mystery, we meditate on the truth that Mary prayed with the apostles and many people converted to Christianity (Acts 1:14) Her power of intersession is truly great: it defeated the Ottoman forces, Russia's Communism, and it will defeat the Devil. Of course, Mary is not the source of this power since God does not depend on any creature for His power. But we cannot deny that She is the most special of all His creatures by virtue of the fact that she is the *Spouse of the Holy Spirit* and the *Mother of God,* and that she exercised her free will when she said "Yes."

THE 4TH GLORIOUS MYSTERY

The Assumption of Mary into Heaven

Mary's trip to Heaven was nonstop, but we might have
layovers on the way there.

The meditative fruit of this mystery is the importance of
cultivating the virtue of *hope* that we, like Mary, shall be
raised into Heaven. The *Catechism of the Catholic Church*
teaches that this form of hope is not a natural or secular
hope, but a form of hope that belongs to a trio, called the
Theological Virtues: Faith, Hope, and Charity.

When we lose hope in temporal efforts, we give up.
Consider a university student who fails several times to pass
an examination in trigonometry, despite paying tutors to
prepare him for the examination or the law school graduate
who fails several attempts at passing the State Bar
Examination; they most likely lose hope of ever passing the
examinations and give up. It's a loss that significantly
changes the direction of one's life.

I know graduate students in philosophy who have never
managed to complete writing their doctoral dissertations;
one of them was clearly brilliant, having received the award
of "Best Undergraduate Student in Philosophy" in his
graduating class at a prestigious university and getting hired
as a teacher by another prestigious university. For some
reason, he couldn't finish his dissertation and thus lost his

teaching position at the university, winding up in a totally different job with the Federal Government. I was pretty sure that he had given up his plans to become a university professor, for when I asked him how his dissertation was going, he replied, "I don't want to discuss it."

What about people who have lost hope, fearing that they have been too sinful to spend eternity with God or because they no longer believe in personal immortality or God's existence? What could make a more fundamental change in one's outlook in life than believing that death means eternal oblivion?

The loss of hope in immortality radically changes one's interpretation and responses to what happens in this life, and, indeed, radically changes the entire culture. Today, we witness the rise of secularism and the decline of Christianity. As I wrote elsewhere:

> "The modern world is secular in that it is godless and thus stands in marked contrast to previous ages. But the meaning of secularism cannot fully be grasped except as a reaction against Christianity. There could never have been secularism if there had first been no Christianity. Hence, although "paganism" and "secularism" are frequently used interchangeably, they are not synonyms; "paganism" is, in fact, a misnomer when applied to the modern world. For the pagans acknowledged the existence of gods and of God, and it is no exaggeration to

say that pagan culture was based on this acknow-ledgment. The Athenians, for example, attributed their legal code to divine origins, and when we read Plato's creation document, the *Timaeus*, what emerges very clearly is the conviction that not only was the universe created by God but that it remains under His providential surveillance.

Secularism, on the contrary, rejects the existence of God and the transcendent, maintaining that human happiness and progress are to be attained by man's own efforts, if they are to be attained at all. The most spectacular example of this view is Marxism, which promises mankind paradise on earth through a rational organization of economic forces. But it is in the *Humanist Manifesto,* which first appeared in the 1930s, that one sees perhaps the most precise and explicit formulations of secularism's view of man and his relation to the rest of the universe. What the philosophy behind this manifesto comes down to is that not only is belief in God and personal immortality unnecessary for happiness and progress, it is antithetical to them."[47]

But atheists do have options, many of them diaphanous in the long run. The first is to do one's best to make life better

---

[47] Raymond Dennehy, *Christian Married Love,* op. cit., pp. 12-13.

for future generations, to wit, make the world more just, peaceful, safe, healthy, interesting, and entertaining, etc.; the second would be to conquer death. Thus, human hope would have its rationale in the knowledge that, until we conquer death, each of us can dismiss the *ennui*, the boredom, that inevitably shadows the realization that death means eternal oblivion by reminding ourselves that we are living and working to make a better world for future generations.

How have we been doing in making the world a better place? Things are better economically in Europe, America, and Asia, but the Stock Market can be a slippery companion. How about health and longevity? A baby born now in the United States can expect to live to be 100 years old. And it looks like we're having increasing success in curing cancer, given, for example, new treatments like immunotherapy.

What are the prospects for world peace? Current (2021) tensions among the United States, Russia, Iran, North Korea, and China do not bode well for a peaceful world, especially when considering the weapons of choice: guided nuclear missiles.

How about conquering death? Good luck with that! A man and woman of the future pronounced "immortal" because science has rendered them impervious to disease and aging would die as surely as any of us today if a building collapsed on them or an auto accident crushed them or a psychotic "who was very angry" shot them along with a gathering of other anonymous human victims. Good-bye life; hello eternal oblivion!

So, until further notice, atheists and materialists will not easily dismiss from consciousness the truth that the prospect of eternal oblivion awaits them. Will they find consolation in the belief that the future generations for whom they are now working to benefit will appreciate the labors of their predecessors?

I suspect not. Why? Because humans are *self-aware* beings, as indicated by the first-person singular pronoun "I". Each of us is a unique center of self-conscious, autonomous being and it is logically impossible to have two humans for whom "I" has the same referent and meaning. Truly, human beings do voluntarily give up their lives for others. Consider, for example, Charles Dickens' novel *A Tale of Two Cities* in which one character, Sydney Carton, pretends to be another person, Charles Darnay, and chooses to be executed in Darnay's place. "Carton first appears as a cynical drunkard who serves as a legal aide to a London barrister. He is secretly in love with Lucie Manette, whose French émigré husband, Charles Darnay, physically resembles Carton. This coincidence enables Carton to stand in for Darnay, who has been sentenced to die on the guillotine. By this act Carton gives meaning to his misspent life." Carton's words are memorable: "It is a far, far better thing that I do, than I have ever done; it is a far, far better rest that I go to than I have ever known."[48]

In my chapter on Christ's agony in Gethsemane recall that I address the various reasons why people risk their lives –e.g., defending their county or rescuing people in danger— and the reasons why they take their own lives—e.g., loss of meaning in one's life or escaping public exposure for horrible crimes or humiliating behavior. I also note in the same essay: "Suicides often occur following breakups in a relationship, substance abuse, financial problems, evictions, legal troubles, and physical health problems…. According to CDC criteria, over half of those who kill themselves had no known mental health diagnosis."

The above paragraph shows that we should, as *personal beings,* not be too quick to affirm that we would sacrifice our lives for people as impersonal as "future generations." That we easily give money for the poor and sick, to families and individuals whom we don't know and will not be likely ever to meet, requires a quite different psychology from that of living to make a better life for future generations before lapsing into eternal oblivion. On the contrary, Sydney Carton was not living in a foggy world of anonymity, for he knew himself to be a cynical drunkard, but that by masquerading as his friend, Charles Darnay, and going to

---

[48] Charles Dickens, *A Tale of Two Cities,* 1859.

the guillotine instead of Darnay, he could confer meaning on his own otherwise meaningless life. This hope stretched also to Darnay's survival and to the happiness of his wife, Lucie, whom Carton secretly loved.

And what about Mary's hope? She was not simply another human being, but, as I wrote above, the Spouse of the Holy Spirit, to wit, the Spouse of God, and the Mother of God, the Son. Skepticism would drown us were we told that she remained unfazed by it all. Mary was truly the mother of Jesus and surely suffered a mother's grief and anguish as she witnessed His torture and death. So, it was fitting that her assumption into Heaven was a direct flight. The rest of us can expect going to Heaven (if we lead good lives) while hoping to avoid stopovers; but not to worry; our *hope* that we can get to Heaven has Christ's own words for its validation:

"Ask and it will be given to you; seek and you will find; knock and the door will be opened to you. For everyone who asks, receives; and the one who seeks, finds; and to the one who knocks, the door will be opened. Which one of you would hand his son a stone when he asks for a loaf of bread, or a snake when he asks for a fish? If you then, who are wicked, know how to give good gifts to your children, how much more will your heavenly Father give good things to those who ask him. (Matthew 7:7-11, NAB)

The most precious gift, of course, would be getting to Heaven, a reality also validated by Christ's own words: "Jesus said to them, 'The children of this age marry and are given in marriage; but those who are deemed worthy to attain to the coming age and to the resurrection of the dead neither marry nor are given in marriage. They can no longer die, for they are like angels; and they are the children of God because they are the ones who will rise. That the dead will rise even Moses made known in the passage about the bush, when he called 'Lord' the God of Abraham, the God of Isaac, and the God of Jacob; and he is not God of the dead, but of the living, for to him all are alive.'" (Luke 20:34-38, NAB)

THE 5TH GLORIOUS MYSTERY

The Coronation of Mary Queen of Heaven

That Christ crowned Mary Queen of Heaven is well-explained by Fr. William G. Most, who writes,

"The solidly theological reasons for her title of Queen are expressed splendidly by Pius XII, in his Radio message to Fatima, Bendito seja (AAS 38. 266): 'He, the Son of God, reflects on His heavenly Mother the glory, the majesty and the dominion of His kingship, for, having been associated to the King of Martyrs in the unspeakable work of human Redemption as Mother and cooperator, she remains forever associated to Him, with a practically unlimited power, in the distribution of the graces which flow from the Redemption. Jesus is King throughout all eternity by nature and by right of conquest: through Him, with Him, and subordinate to Him, Mary is Queen by grace, by divine relationship, by right of conquest, and by singular choice [of the Father]. And her kingdom is as vast as that of her Son and God, since nothing is excluded from her dominion.'"[49]

---

[49] William G. Most, "Queen of Heaven and Earth," excerpted and adapted from Theology 523: Our Lady in Doctrine and Devotion, 1994.
https://www.ewtn.com/catholicism/teachings/queen-of-heaven-and-earth-189

I've observed, in addition, several times so far in this book, and it's worth observing again, that the Holy Spirit (God) impregnated Mary, which makes her *God's Spouse*, and that she thus gave birth to Christ (also God), which makes her the *Mother of God*.

If being both the Spouse of God and the Mother of God do not pass muster as equivalent to Queenship of Heaven, I don't know what would. Mary herself is a creature of God and thus infinitely below Him, as are all creatures. Bluntly put, she has no power that does not come from God. Yet, her intercessory powers must exceed those of all other creatures in Heaven.

And in the discussion of the 3rd Glorious Mystery, it was fitting to dwell on the power of her prayers for us when, for example, she prayed with the Apostles in the early Church, interceded for the Christian militia on the eve of their sea battle with the Ottoman Empire at Lepanto, and prayed with Christians the world over for the demise of Communism in Russia. Also, I understand that, next to the Holy Sacrifice of the Mass, the Church regards Mary's Rosary as the most important devotion.

God had a purpose for Mary that flows from her reality as Mother of God and Spouse of the Holy Spirit. For example, unlike Mary, Christ is both human and divine; He is God but also like us in all things except sin. Mary is solely human. When Christ crowned Mary "Queen of Heaven," did He also intend to impress upon us the *accessibility* of God and Heaven by presenting and exalting Mary as the "Queen of Heaven" although a total human being? She, a human being, and not divine, had parental authority over her son, Christ, even when what was at stake went beyond temporal matters to His divine mission. For example, at the marriage feast in Cana, when the supply of wine had gone dry, she called her Son's attention to the problem—"They have no wine." She asked, and He initially objected—"Woman, my time has not yet come."—and then, He did what she asked. He miraculously made more wine out of water.

Granted, the Lord answers all our prayers, sometimes the answer, for our own good, is "No." Why do we pray to Mary for favors? In the introduction to this book, I quoted the words of Mother Teresa: "You cannot learn this from books, you must experience it in your life, that whatever you ask Our Lady she will do…" I understand that, as Pope St. John Paul II lay bleeding, after the attempted assassination on him, he called to Mother Mary, "Save me." Apparently, it is not unknown for a soldier lying on the battlefield, wounded and defenseless, and realizing that the enemy soldier standing before him is about to kill him will call out "Mother" or "Mama."

Made in the USA
Monee, IL
21 April 2021

66391036R00094